GW00370491

EDITORIAL

BERNARDINE EVARISTO

In 1912 (The) *Poetry Review* emerged out of an earlier poetry magazine called *The Poetical Gazette* (1909). The *Review*'s first Editor, Harold Monro, had this to say about 'women poets' in his introduction to the May issue of that year: "He (Man) has represented Woman so adequately in poetry that there seemed scarcely any call for her to represent herself. Now at last, however, some change is taking place. Woman, late though it be, is becoming conscious of herself. Her awakening begins in a startled blinking of her eyes, an exclamation: 'What am I?' It proceeds in the helpless call: 'I am no worse than Man. I am no longer his slave'; then she throws up wild arms, and smashes windows."

That same year the Suffragettes progressed from chaining themselves to railings to planting bombs, acts of arson and, yes, smashing windows. Monro remained unconvinced: "Despite all emancipation, Woman still lies in a garden and we must receive her verses gift-wise, as we might some fine broidery. She will play with a fancy as lovingly as with a child; she enjoys delicacy in her verse, and soft light shades: she loves especially a gentle hopefulness."

I wonder what this Edwardian man would make of this issue of the *Review*? No gardens, flowers, butterflies or what I call 'pigeon poems' to be found in these pages. As Guest Editor I am not only a woman (and in a hundred years there have been only three women editors, Muriel Spark, Tracey Warr and Fiona Sampson), but a black woman at that.

I was shocked and delighted to be invited to guest edit Britain's oldest and most 'establishment' poetry publication as I don't consider myself a poetry insider and can usually be found kicking up a fuss outside the castle walls. I decided to demonstrate inclusivity by example (as opposed to tokenism) and to embrace a wide range of voices. I put a call out for work that engages with society, culture(s), politics and that slippery old thing called identity.

The result is an issue that includes many poets of colour and twenty-five women poets. I also feature several openly 'queer' poems. I sought originality, variety and re-readability. I wanted more formal experimentation than I could find, although some of what I found breaks new ground, and I found some exciting and riskily exuberant prose poem puzzles, layered with abundant meanings and ways of reading.

My aim was to only publish poems by poets who have never before had a poem featured in the magazine. (I almost achieved this.) Some of these poets are new to poetry, some are still only in their early twenties, while others have been around for a while but this is their *Review* debut. Essays were commissioned to explore the relationship between various kinds of 'culture' and poetry, negotiating contested labels and reductive groupings, alongside reviews of several anthologies that move us from the parochial to the international.

I commissioned Jay Bernard to produce a bold, provocative cover and was thrilled with her explosive, anarchic kaleidoscope with its riff on multiples, on hearing and with several African images – surely a first for the *Review*.

I came up with the title, 'Offending Frequencies', because of its imaginative and interpretive scope. It is the pitch at which sound becomes unbearable – in this context depending on the wave length of the hearer (ie what is tolerated/what is not); *hertz* = the internalised hurts and the external perpetrators of repeated hurts: war, rape, persecution, corruption, intolerance, exploitation, brutalisation, family, death; it is the compression of intensely felt experience into the sound waves of poetry and the decompression of intense experience through the catharsis of poetry; there are poems here of sonic protest and unrest (sub-sonic and ultra sonic *equally* valued) as we explore the frequencies of our *selves*: the reverberation of disparate poets' voices *amplified* into an acoustic wall of words and sound.

I am amused that Monro could never have predicted what our country, our society, became, who we are, what we choose to write. The poems in the early incarnation of the *Review* have not aged well. Nor will most of the poetry of our times. Who cares? All art is ephemeral unless history proves otherwise. We cannot predict the future.

A hundred years ago 'Negroes' were considered primitive at best, savages at worst; India was still the 'jewel in the crown'; to be queer meant to feel a 'bit poorly'; most poetry rhymed and anyone predicting the internet age would have been dispatched to an asylum.

Would Monro's generation be turning in their graves at this polyphonic-poetic-cacophony of our contemporary age? I certainly hope so.

Bernardine Evaristo's books include fiction and verse fiction. Her new novel will be published by Penguin in 2013. An editor and literary critic, she teaches creative writing at Brunel University and for UEA-Guardian Masterclasses. She has won and judged several literary awards, and in 2012 was Chair of the Caine Prize for African Fiction, the Commonwealth Short Story Award and she founded the Brunel University African Poetry Prize. She was made an MBE in 2009. www.bevaristo.com

Contents

Volume 102:4 Winter 2012

Epilogue

CENTREFOLD

REVIEWS

POEMS

❧

I glimpsed, below **where**
swirling swarms of hoodoo-voodoo priests, fetish **fishgutfunk**
witch-doctors, obeah men, pocomania roots women **fumed**
at their muddied fount. Undeterred making headway, **furiously**.

– Dorothea Smartt

Jacqueline Saphra
Getting into Trouble

Mr Giles said he didn't want the school used as a political jousting ground and made me take the pro-abortion poster down, although I explained patiently that the ancient Romans didn't mind it, that the church was okay with it in the 13th Century until quickening (when, they said, the soul enters the body), and the statute books condoned it.

Michelle, who was a Born Again, insisted life was ensouled even before conception; Clare believed that once the foetus was viable it had a right to exist, my mother said she didn't believe in the primacy of the unborn, and I sat in biology wondering if I had a soul, and if I did, where it was. I daydreamed of knitting needles, coat hangers and permanganate.

After my mother came back from hospital – unharmed, grateful and political, only to find that my stepfather had spent her emergency money on canvasses and Carlsberg and dinner with that woman in Portobello Road, she sent me straight to the doctor, gratuitously, as it happened, to get myself a Dutch cap.

My boyfriend who was stupid but useful told all his friends I was a virgin and forced me to see Close Encounters of the Third Kind three times and listen to nothing but Genesis, which I preferred to The Sex Pistols, because I never believed there was No Future, not when my mother was, at least for now, empty-wombed and full of soul, as she stirred a pot of her famous lentil soup, not yet tied by blood to the man she loved.

Jemma Borg
The lover of Amazonian catfish

They say it is rational to turn inwards
to your obsession, to wake to it and love it,
but I tell you, when the storms come down
and the rain falls like stones onto the river,
I can't open my eyes to its sting.
      My childless hip

starts up its ache along the beltline
where I hook my thumb. Then the waves come
up over the canoe as if to drown me
within reach of shore, and I have to think
of where to jump to should a caiman
        land at my feet.

But it passes. And then, above the cataracts,
where the water eases and takes the rain
like a boiling mirror instead:
always a greater treasure of fish,
and then a greater one still in the tiny creeks
        we call *igarapés*

and into that slow-moving catch
as bizarre as a netted dream, I sink
my heart's current, the lines of its wonder
tracing the body of my fish
from the promontory of its ancient head
        to its long and breakable tail.

Valerie Laws
Keepers

(2012 doll 'reborning,'
1859 post-mortem photography.)

I am putting in his eyes,
I am painting in her eyes.
'Adorable Arctic Blue', optical grade
Acrylic, guaranteed not to fade.
Inked onto dead, closed lids,
Her soulless pupils gaze into my lens.
I hand-root his lashes, micro-root his brows,
Her lashes, I'll draw later; and a white dot
For the spark of life, onto the ambrotype plate.
The soft fine mohair swirling on his scalp
Is inserted over many hours. Perfection takes time.
The exposure takes time. My subjects
Never fidget, but gravity tugs them out of true,
The earth impatient for them. Even ice
Can't keep time still. Every 'Forever Nursery'
Reborn baby, I care for as my own.

Nine days dead, this child.
My lamp begins to warm and wake her. Gagging,
My nostrils plugged with menthol, I recreate her
Living likeness, preserve her mother's motherhood,
Proof of the child, the future, she once had.
Packing plastic beads into limbs and torso, I weight
Each newborn to sag just right in the crook of my arm.
I brace her dead weight upright, the iron frame
Hidden by the frock her mama was keeping for best.
I strive for that perfect reborn, for absolute realism,
Use 'Genesis' heat-set paints in stippled layers
For moist lips, milk spots, tastebuds, the flush of sleep.
Her image blooms upon the plate; I add a faint rose tint
To cheeks last flushed with fever. A special order, this,
From a photo of a baby grown or gone to heaven.
Last, I slip into his breast the flutter of a beating heart
(Batteries included), send him to his new Mummy,
Forever young, *forever safe.*

Richard Scott
Trainee Priest at Rochuskapelle

Saint Sebastian stands covered with the hunger-cloth –
a hooded detainee from off the seminary television.
We must give up the sight of him to focus on the bare Easter altar.

Good Friday I will lift the veil, search his face for a clue of agony.
I don't believe the sculptor's lie, he cannot be at peace.
He is like me, young when he gave himself to God.

While the priests are diluting wine
I would have him tug off his sack, step down, walk...
I will lie him across my lap, pull out the cock-feathered arrows,

wash the holes in his body, sew them up
with my mother's darning needle, ask if I will be forgiven
for wanting his delicate blood on my fingers.

But Sebastian is carved, I have traced the chisel's evidence
with my thumb. I know my thread can't heal –
he and his arrows are of the same body of Milanese oak.

There is no stop where either wound or weapon begin –
our devotion is a perpetual hurt. I am like him,
young, bound for a lifetime of suffering behind cloth.

Ahimsa Timoteo Bodhrán
Honig

Our love sweet, brought to temple for High Holy Days, dipped honey into apple and feed you, something else your mouth waters, swallows, arms wrapped round—*date vuelta, papi, date, dame, dámelo, dame*—this queer synagogue, so white. *Feed me.* A book neither of us can read, always losing our place. *Dulce.* Ashkenazi asphyxia, a dyke who does not know how to shut up. Something to parch our hunger, feed our thirst. *Tengo hambre, papi, tengo sed.* Durst und Hunger, und vielleicht mehr, weiß ich nicht. Weiß. Ich. Nicht. *Gracias, mijo, gracias.* Agua, after blessing. A thin wafer, tired knees, Latin (services), oil that could be used for food, or heating one's home. What we give up for Lent, better life in América. Vatican II. Chocolate. What we are truly looking forward to—that night.

Prayers from a kneeling position. I supplicate. Suffocate. You are my breath, votive after donation, lit, and lying (beneath you), my greatest sins, I have nothing to tell the priest. I let someone go in before me, close the door for them, listen, I have not been to confession since I came out of the closet. *The blessing of the throat. New confirmation name.* Eight good, long years.

Before the year of white, move further into the religion, a time when I am still eating meat. Before Oakland and grad school, our last supper, over hummus and tabouli, time away from your white lover, my female one. Valencia pre-dot.com. I believe you ordered the lamb.

You tap my head against the thin wall of the kitchen. We are two Catholic boys in search of something deeper.

Richard Scott
Public Toilets in Regent's Park

The men here are bird-footed
feathering past the attendant's two-way mirror
unperturbed by the colonizing micro-organisms –
bulleidia   cobetia   shigellosis

sliming across the yellowed groutings,
the fist-deep pool of brackish water
quivering in the U bend, the tile that reads
for information on venereal disease telephone 01. . .

All for the thrill of placing their knees
on the piss-stained cold, the iris shimmering
behind a hand-carved glory hole,
a beautiful cock unfolding like a swans' neck
from the Harris Tweed of a city gent's suit.

Whispers, gasps of contact echo
inside each nested cubicle. But careful –
the prying attendant will rattle
her bucket and mop if she spies four shoes.
Our men disperse suddenly, as mallards from the face of a pond.

Ahimsa Timoteo Bodhrán
How to Make Love to a Dying Rican

1. Remember he is still living.

2. Remember you, too, will die.

3. Try not to rush either.

4. Kiss his lips full of medicine.
    Rub his back full of knots.

5. Remember he wants you alive;
    don't be foolish.

6. Realize you will both become statistics.

7. Remember the way his face looked
    in the movie he made. Remember
    it in the one you are now making.

8. Tell him he can play any role.

9. Inscribe in memory
    the sound of his voice, feel of
    his hands on your chest, waist,
    hips. The trace of his finger across your
    lips, yours in the recess
    of his ass.

10. Keep rum and candy
    nearby. They keep the gods happy.

11. Tell him you will visit
    in the next life, and this island
    will again be filled
    with trees.

12. In the canoe of our own
    making, we travel upstream.

    Fill the hollow of his hull.

    Husk the corn from his frame.

13. Cacique dance.

    Bless his limbs with flight.

Rody Gorman
from Sweeney

Smoothshining Studbeadbuttons

His regalia was like this: a filmy silk albshirt
Next to his brightwhite handsomebodyskin
And a royal ruched satin girdle around it
Which Conall gave him the day of the battle
As a gift of fealty and a lilacpurple tuniclayer
Coloured with warpclose stripselvage well plaitwoven
With delightbeautiful findrinny gold goldburnished
In layers of dearsmooth gemstones of carbunclescabmesh-husk
From one headend of that stripselvage to the other
With arcbillowloops of silkvelveteen over
Smoothshining studbeadbuttons to rallydamclose
And open it and a glebecuttingtroutspeckling
Of all whitebright moneysilver
Everywhichway and every trajectorymountaindogpass
He would go and a needlenarrow spearpointhard
On that layertunic, two exceedingly long
Broadflatsurfaced splinterspears in his hands,
A troutpox-speckledthanksyellow buffalo-hornbugle
Wingshield on his topvineback
And a fistgolden sword on his left chestside.

Warsan Shire
What We Have

Our men do not belong to us. Even my own father, left one afternoon, is not mine. My brother is in prison, is not mine. My uncles, they go back home and they are shot in the head, are not mine. My cousins, stabbed in the street for being too – or not – enough, are not mine.

Then the men we try to love, say we carry too much loss, wear too much black, are too heavy to be around, much too sad to love. Then they leave and we mourn them too. Is that what we're here for? To sit at kitchen tables, counting on our fingers the ones who died, those who left and the others who were taken by the police, or by drugs, or by illness or by other women. It makes no sense. Look at your skin, her mouth, these lips, those eyes, my God, listen to that laugh. The only darkness we should allow into our lives is the night, and even then, we have the moon.

Roger Robinson
Trinidad Gothic

Some of the women in Point Ligoure had already been arrested
for seasoning their husbands' food with a pinch of cement powder.
A stone grew. Grit in an oyster. Chalk in a rooster's gizzard.
Within two weeks they lay dead with a wolf's stone in their stomachs.

The women all had a good reason for this mode of murder
and passed the method on to other women with the same reason.
But alas, too many of the men of Point Ligoure died all at once
which prompted an investigation, which led to a mass autopsy.

They peeled back the flaps of their stomachs to find stone after stone.
Which led to aunties, grandmothers and girlfriends being led
away in daydresses and handcuffs as the other women looked on.
But a clever woman in Point Ligoure has found a new way.

If you leave an iron out overnight and before sunrise
you pummel the base of that iron with a slap to the sole
of his feet, you will cause an instant untraceable heart attack.
And so, this night, you will find a dozen irons glinting in moon's light.

Nabila Jameel
Visiting Time

An amoeba-shaped stain
on the bleached sheet
beneath your swollen thighs
increases in size.

The curtains enclose you; the midwife
whose hands you know so well
helps to latch your new-born to your
burning breast.

With each suck, your womb contracts.
You cry. She thinks you're in pain,
passing you a pain-killer
on a surgical silver tray.

You do not hear your child,
only the cooing voices
of fathers, in Ward 5.

Suzanne Conway
Sherbet

At 3am, a knock. It's not my house they want,
a string of men for the peroxide blonde next door.
They wait, wolves watching quarters of moon.

When I was nine, men like these came
as I collected blackberries, while my parents,
at home, drank themselves empty.

They dipped into me like I was sherbet,
as my friends spun buttercups,
searched for yellow under their chins.

Ivy Alvarez
from The Everyday English Dictionary

L

loricate:

> I could not walk long with it
> assaulted on all sides as I was.
> A castle tries to be impregnable
> with slits in the walls   to see out
> I had a lightless feeling   wore my armour
> went into battle daily   mended breaches nightly
> waited for peace   for truce

lucarne:

> innumerable insects drawn to me
> clustered by the grass and clinging to wallpaper
> swinging curtains do not disturb them
> outside   the far river
> trees breathing out   the wind

lucubrate:

> between floorboard cracks
> I watched her needle and thread
> mend and mend
> a dim sky turns dimmer
> the oil in the wick seeps upwards
> slaking the flame
>   her face   cracked with shadow

luculent:

> who will remember them now
> their small wings   bellies full of glowing
> all through the papery night   the fireflies' invisible ink

Katie Hale
Secret

Against all odds, we keep her
locked in the dark space under the house
to try to stop the distortion of her face,
to keep us (in some way) safe. It's a joint effort.
You bind her hands in complex knots
(it has been suggested she has the ability to pick locks),
chain one ankle to the ground.
I cover her with a blanket to muffle her sounds
of mewling pity, her moans of malnutrition.
We feed her as seldom as possible.
We stop inviting the neighbours round,
change all our privacy settings to invisible.
We cut the phone line, lock the door
and nail the floorboards over our mouths.

Simon McCormack
Navigating by Hang-ups

A hand-me-down girl lends her body to the boys
on the estate, love-bites like graffiti on a wall, but etched
with a compass on a toilet door – a bar-gate of five,

with dates and hearts. Her route home is beaten
through a weed-spangled playing field – beyond that
she grows up with mum and six older brothers,

eats fast, plays hop-scotch between a lamp-post
and the chippy, disappears into a maze of black paths,
link-fence and security doors scrawled with sharpie tags.

A red head, stick thin and strike-wild, she finds her way,
flares for this rough strip of a lad, the spit of her dad, pours out
a faultless heat. He fancies himself in her light,

rolls her between finger and thumb – names her freckles
after stars, places constellations on her shoulders:
Orion's Belt, The Plough, a birthmark in the small of her back

becomes the Horsehead Nebula. They flatten the grass, clatter, sag
briefly, snipped marionettes half-dressed and unmapped.

Abegail Morley
Summer's End in Hackney

So that she might go unnoticed, she doesn't turn
on the sitting-room light when the street lights sputter,

announce evening in a sudden gust of white
that catches out the rain. She wonders if it's okay

to start drinking at four, winter nights creep in
ever earlier. In the kitchen she greets the fridge:

they blink at each other for a minute –
she reaches for the wine, grabs it like it's ripe on the vine,

the Veneto sun freckling her arms, and the 50 kilo basket
dragging her backwards into the hot earth.

She presses the bottle to her cheek, remembers how
each grape was too low to squat for, too low not to stoop,

and how she spent that holiday, stretched the full-length
of his bed watching the first light distil the dawn,

splash through the shutters, ooze across the room.

Katrina Naomi

Step-father graph

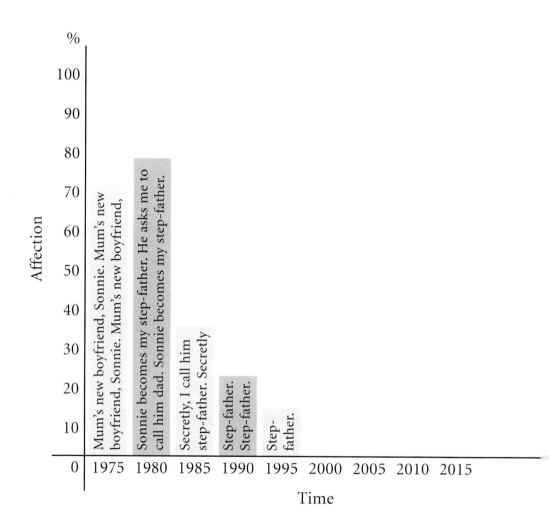

Katrina Naomi
Willpower

He couldn't say no to a fried egg sarnie, smeared with Daddy's sauce,
eating two as a snack. Other days, our stepfather barely ate,
yet was up at 4, his engine running, as he lifted truckloads of turf.
He was always jumpy, mostly in a temper in our front room,
all hemmed in by the giant sofa. When he didn't eat, he was worse;
resenting the lack of food, his 17 stones, me, the eldest,
who ate what she wanted and stayed slim, resenting the hour-long drive.
And he couldn't eat or sleep after work, sprawled on the couch
in silk pyjama bottoms, lolloping breasts bared as he flicked
between channels, riffled through *The Sport* and *The People*.
He bought his slimming tablets – speed, amphetamines, whizz –
in bulk in Thailand. Gave my sister two when she said she'd put on weight.
She skipped breakfast, lunch and tea, her brown eyes buzzed through school,
her heart sprinted for days. She learnt to say no to his pills, his fried egg sarnies.
His moods darkened, though he never hit us like he did our mother.
I once told him to punch me and his ice blue eyes screwed into mine,
acid in the crease of his lips, his flaccid face too close, spittle flying.
I didn't hear his words, just stood until that wave of rage crashed,
or he caught the tv's whine of motor racing and heaved his frame
back to the sofa and I'd escape, another drug surging through my veins –
sometimes hate, sometimes pity, but always cut with fear.

Dorothea Smartt
Headway

> *down near the jetty where fishgutfunk fumed furiously*
> – Anthony Joseph, *The African Origins of UFO*

The time was ripe. Heal me, lead me willingly **down,**
out past deceits, to our own brand of salvation. The **near-**
east, far-east, western, native American, the aboriginal, **the**
'Egyptian' wells of oneness, missing a voice. Out on the **jetty**
of my life so far, I'd had to wonder. I glimpsed, below **where**
swirling swarms of hoodoo-voodoo priests, fetish **fishgutfunk**
witch-doctors, obeah men, pocomania roots women **fumed**
at their muddied fount. Undeterred making headway, **furiously**.

Rody Gorman
from Suibhne

Soldier's Heart

When the battlebatallions on every both sides encounterfought
They braylowroared like a vast herd
Of stagoxchampions back and forth
And hammerpummelled three heavy hakashouts on high.
When Sweeney heard those exalt great cries
And their sounds and outcropreverberations in the trancenebulae
Of non sky heaven and in the vaultrafter
Of the firm aments he trylooked up in the hallucinationspheresky
And was filled with war-goddessbattle-fury
And darkness and sudden violent madness
And flutterloitering and floathovering and fumblerestlessness
And double unsteadyrestlessness and strifemalice for every place
Where he used to be and belovedcharitylove for every place he was not.
His branchfingers were deadened, his legfeet trembled,
His heart quickened, his bodily senses and perceptions
Were cleave-subdued, he lost the power of vision,
His arms fell naked from his hands
And he went with the wordcurses of Ronan
In double woodpanicmadness and goblin likeness
Like every tinywildserpentinsectbeast of the air.

Steve Tasane
Rats In The Attic

The neighbours are at it again,
their scattergun domestic shakes the foundations,
setting off the howl of a dog
whimpering in nearby neglect.

A rumble of revellers nightbus
over the speedbumps of his slumber.
The dull chunter of a free-range alcoholic
and the pickaxe wit of overnight track workers
keep time with the pounding crunk of his inner panic.

The pre-dawn echo of yesterday's complaints
is hectored away by the nagging advice
of an elder brother; lecturing from the grave,
on how best to cope with the voices.

Gas bags, rattling in his head.
Angry bed bugs.
Hush now. Baby needs his sleep,
for tomorrow will be war.

Edward Doegar
A Gentile Visits The East Coast

After Lowell

So much for a gentle beginning. Married life started
with a trip to the in-laws as soon as we landed.
Three nights alone with my wife's
family, the first time we'd seen them
since the wedding. Payback for their hand
in the honeymoon. Come Tuesday I was heartily
relieved to leave their shitty
put-downs behind. Afterwards, we visited sites
of cultural interest on the drive
down to Dulles, through Brooklyn Heights,
through the detour of Atlantic City,
through Philly with its purposeless streets,
to D.C. where we did the Holocaust Museum
and then didn't fuck for a week.

Dorothea Smartt
Reader, I married Him

Reader, I married him.
A son with his father's name,
loving a man twice his age
hiding from dem men that kill
he las' 'fren' – and chop-he
widda a machete! Slice scarring he face
impairing he eyes (like a Mr. Rochester)
but not mine, I could see a way, clear-clear.

Reader, I married him
so he could lef outta JA. Take refuge
in my British citizenship.
My redundant heterosex right
to marry any man – so I flew to Bim,
to do it beachside, tropical style –
at least in the photos
that would serve as proof.

Reader, I married him
My best man? His lover, gave me away.
Was wedding planner, witness
and his wedding night delight.
Man enough to cover every detail
of our act. Rehearsing Junior
in his role. For this was a political act:
I was the life-boat, love boat.

Reader, I married him,
this young guy half my age.
The Bajan registrar looked weary
at another 'rent-a-dread' giving
'stella-her-groove-back'!
I was a politically incorrect (act):
bewitch, turn-head tourist trapped
by his honey eyes. Glazed, by my island man.

Reader, I married him.
I was confident, self-assured, but
still feigning new love coyness.
He was all fingers and thumbs,
dumb in the presence of civic authority.
Me, the blushing brown skin bride,
who produced the rings, asked
his lover for the wedding bands.

Reader, I married him – for love
of our humanity. Arms entwined,
we sipped each other's champagne.
Clutching me between Sandy Lane's columns,
lover now photographer, sneaking kisses.
Reader, I married him, played a part
for a JA brother. To escape erroneous outrage.
Reader I, married him, with our 'tainted' love

we said – "I do".

Sophie Mayer

An Elegy for the Sonnet
as Instrument of Torture

So, Wyatt, you felt guilty, did you? Guilt dribbling
down the line of your body like
come leaking from your courtier mouth. You
didn't swallow. Couldn't. What was the etiquette,
then, anyway, amidst the farthingales and codpieces?
Did your tongue dance a volta
with the clitoris of the king's mistress?
HBO says so, but TV's a reliable guide to fuck-all,
and certainly not to fucking. But there's a Tudor
Kama Sutra not quite encoded – I'm certain, and who's
to contradict me – in Shakespeare's sonnets
and in yours: a diagrammed manual
of swan's-wing hair torture, needle-pricked
play piercing, studded collars, whip-smart naked hunts,
cockringing, double blindfolds,
precise stiletto stabs to the breast and groin. Oh, how
you all loved torture, falling under it, tumbling
to the enseamèd bed for a thumbscrew. Our inheritance
from you: a mouthful of crown jewels,
a snail trail of slipped identities and dirty linen,
all buckled to a verse form that plays
daisy chains with rhymed pairs (legs
entwined in exquisite crucifixions),
whose ecstatic utter shudder is its
quietus: auto-poetic asphyxiation.

Charlotte Ansell
Where they burn books...

That was but a prelude; where they burn books, they will
ultimately burn people also. – Heinrich Heine, 1933, Germany

Off Ferham Rd,
the terraces are pimpled with satellite dishes,
scarred by boarded windows, broken glass
doors are open to the street laying the innards bare,
kameez and jeans lift in the breeze
on a rash of washing lines;
like garish flags over unloved streets.
Gangs of no one's children,
with grubby faces and wide grins
gather round the prize
of an abandoned buggy,
a discarded tyre,
the latest influx is Slovakian; kids
stopping in an outbreak of stares when we pass,
they don't ask, they know.
We also don't belong.

In America Pastor Terry Jones threatens to burn
100 copies of the Qur'an;
the English Defence League invites him to the UK.

December 2010 on Channel Four news,
an Imam from the Luton mosque
attended by the Stockholm bomber,
in muted tones despairs, "Could I have done more?
could I have got alongside him?
his words were of extremity,
but not terrorism.
I challenged all his distorted view of Islam
and thought that was the end of it."
But on ITN and in *The Sun*, it's only bombs.

At home, another match is held to a box,
as the body of Laura Wilson is found floating
in the canal at Holmes,
half a mile from my daughter's primary.
Neighbours who've lived here more than a generation
don't speak the language of belonging;
going to school together didn't breed trust.
An unholy marriage
of Jeremy Kyle and X Factor Saturdays
with Asian hip hop, Al Jazeera,

a tension that predates Laura's murder;
if she had only stayed quiet
but not the first time a married Muslim man
broke rank, slept with what he might call
any slag *kuffar* looking for a way out,
any girl who thought
a baby would make him neglect
family, culture and Allah
but she wasn't one of the chosen ones,
the few English girls in eastern dress,
brown chubby boys on their hips.
So even if his guilt was no more than lust,
he still added more volumes to the blaze,

more excuses
because the BNP will get hold of this.
Will twist this ugly crime into votes,
will offer her family a plasma TV
new carpets for upstairs,
poverty, fury and grief
a heady mix; the streets now electric
as emotions crackle and spit.

'Do Not cross' tape hatches
ground by the canal,
outside school I keep my head down,
silence pools between small groups
where words are not bridges;
muttered behind hands they clog the air,
fat white girls with prams
stub out their fags, chivvy their kids,
Pakistani men strut from their
Toyotas, Nissans,
I don't get the nuances, just
trying to find a place round here to fit.
But Urdu slang in school books gets scribbled over,
some Yorkshire lasses cover old tattoos with a veil,
swap nights on the beer for a demure piety.

At the school Nativity
more than half the school are Muslim,
reciting the Christmas story,
it seems odd to make them.
I'm grateful when Sky's mum
sits next to me until she complains that Sky,
with a tea towel round her head
is being turned into a *paki*,
my shocked silence must seem complicit
to the Muslim mums in the row behind
as a time honoured primary school tradition
becomes something more malign.

And I think I can hear the scrape of a match,
the whisper of sacred pages
as the flames begin to catch.

whosoever

BY JAY BERNARD

DID YOU HAVE CARNAL KNOWLEDGE?

I DID.

I DID NOT

WAS THAT KISS AGAINST THE ORDER OF NATURE?

DID YOU LIE WITH YOUR BROTHER IN ARMS?

FOR WHOSOEVER HAS KNOWLEDGE OF HIM OR HER, OR PERMITS KNOWLEDGE OF HIMSELF OR HERSELF AND SHALL BE LIABLE TO.

WE WILL MAKE A EUNUCH OF YOU, YET

I DID

I DID NOT.

NO

FOR WHOSOEVER TALKS WITH THEM GENTLY, IS GUILTY OF A.

I AM

ARE YOU LIVING ON OR RECEIVING THE PROCEEDS?

NO

DID YOU STAND UNDER ONE COVER WITH A WOMAN NOT RELATED BY CONSANGUINIT

FOR WHOSOEVER WAKES WITH A NAME ON THEIR LIPS, REACHES IN THE MORNING FOR THE BODY THEY DREAMED OF SHALL RECEIVE.

100 LASHES

IT WAS

WAS HER HAND ON YOUR HAND?

YES

75 LASHES

WE NEARLY TOUCHED.

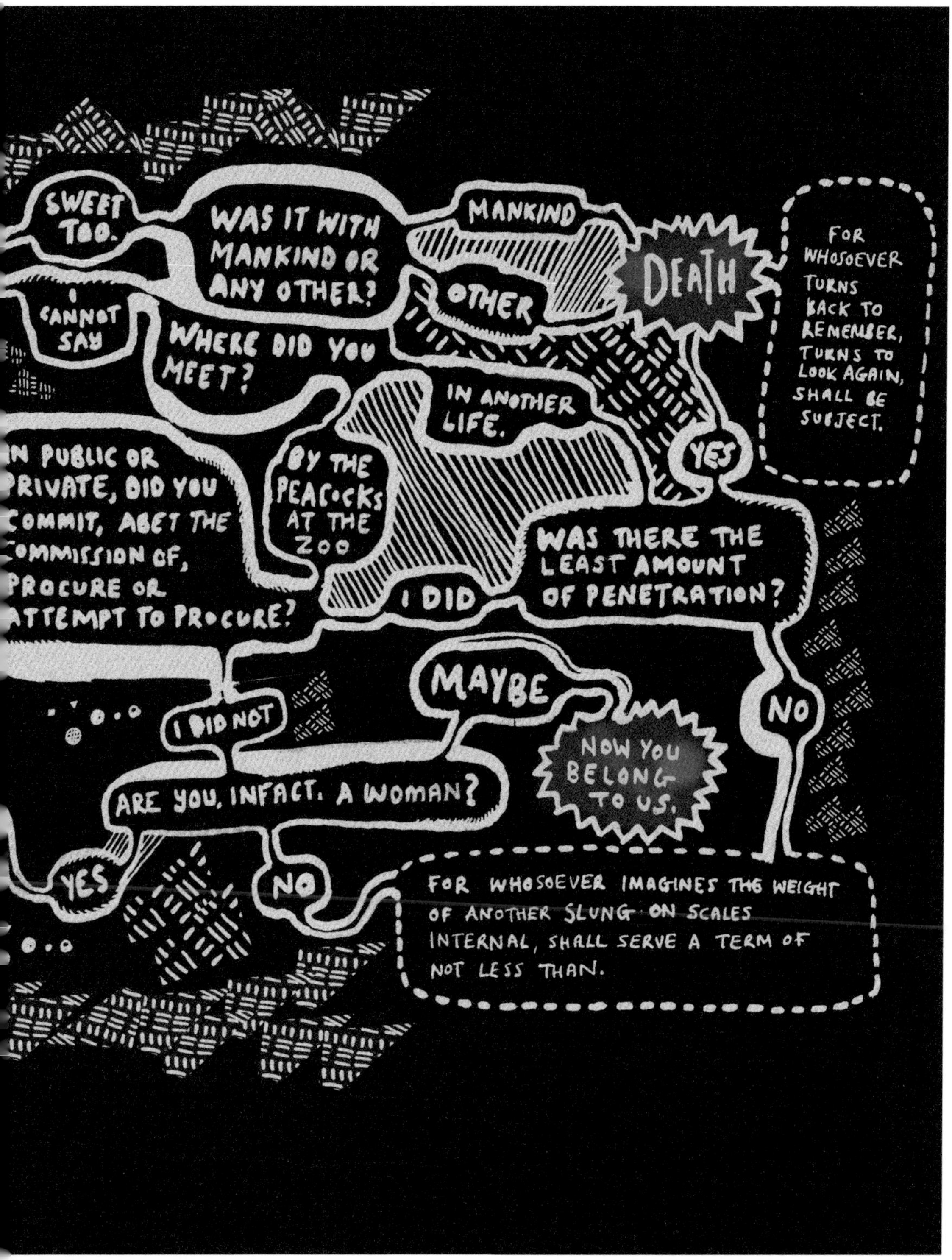

SWEET TOO.
I CANNOT SAY
WAS IT WITH MANKIND OR ANY OTHER?
MANKIND
OTHER
DEATH
FOR WHOSOEVER TURNS BACK TO REMEMBER, TURNS TO LOOK AGAIN, SHALL BE SUBJECT.
WHERE DID YOU MEET?
IN ANOTHER LIFE.
YES
BY THE PEACOCKS AT THE ZOO
IN PUBLIC OR PRIVATE, DID YOU COMMIT, ABET THE COMMISSION OF, PROCURE OR ATTEMPT TO PROCURE?
I DID
WAS THERE THE LEAST AMOUNT OF PENETRATION?
MAYBE
NO
I DID NOT
NOW YOU BELONG TO US.
ARE YOU, INFACT, A WOMAN?
YES
NO
FOR WHOSOEVER IMAGINES THE WEIGHT OF ANOTHER SLUNG ON SCALES INTERNAL, SHALL SERVE A TERM OF NOT LESS THAN.

Tolu Ogunlesi
@TEXT

gbolohun kan le ba oro je, gbolohun kan naa le tun oro se – Yoruba proverb

conman of
inventor of

mis(s)tress 👍Like

CON
[419]
TEXT

[**RT @toluogunlesi:**
"I think the Minister of Information
is a careless talker.
He talks very carelessly.
He did not think properly."
Sen. Pres. David Mark]

TEXT
pre-
TEXT [0702 500 1129: whr r u @ i nd 2 tk 2 u!]

&

of

murderer × Unfollow

slave-master/
equal opportunity misspeller/
mindful that while words may
sometimes be
misunderestimated/ they should
never be misplaced/ never
allowed out of sight...

outa sight = outa meanin':

slaves   love-making slaves   in   master-bedrooms
slaves making beds   love-bed   in-bed   rooms

a n d t h e n i n e v i t a b l y
piling   piling
piling   piling
piling   piling
piling   piling
and then, inevitably,

piling onto the boats... // *row, row, row your boat | gently down the atlantic |*
merrily, merrily, merrily | life is but a dream // **...that brought them here** // *row, row,*

<------- past <------ the <----- for <---- headed <---

dark continents where syn-_-tax is taxed
and silence lent, forcefully, always to sense
bu   tne   ver   n   onsense

Tolu Ogunlesi
Only the dead know

Google Mubi.   Yesterday, or maybe the day before
20+ students, or 46 (+ or -)   lined up,
(to) lie dead, forever.   military uniforms delivered judgement.

twitter *"RT @PoliceNG: Investigations have commenced into this dastardly act, and
we shall leave no stones unturned in our quest to nab the... tmi.me/xFBIU"* 19m

Google Agbor-Abraka Road.   gunmen, nos. unknown, felled 1 cop,
made away with the man   he was paid to protect.

twitter *"RT @PoliceNG: Investigations have commenced into this dastardly act, and
we shall leave no stones unturned in our quest to nab the... tmi.me/xFBIU"* 28m

Google Lagos. Ugo O., 5 days wed   now dead. *They wore police uniforms...*

twitter *"RT @PoliceNG: Investigations have commenced into this dastardly act, and
we shall leave no stones unturned in our quest to nab the... tmi.me/xFBIU"* 36m

only the dead ever know why   they're fucking dead.   Eternity

twitter *"@toluogunlesi: @Nameless Inna lillahi wa inna ilaihi raji'un"* 47m

[...]
In other news, the President takes   another breath, assembles condolese,

facebook *"... with a heart full of sadness and pain that I convey my condolences on
behalf of the Federal Government of Nigeria to the families, friends, associates and
relatives of all those who lost lives in these acts of violence in... [**insert city**] ..."* 47m

and a panel to probe   "the immediate & remote causes of the
                                     insecurity..."

Ugo O: Ugo Ozuah, murdered in Lagos on the night of Thursday 20 September
"Surely we belong to God and to Him shall we return." *Holy Qur'an*

Marvin Thompson
Famous

The phone zooms into spreading blood, three Syrians stretched still
as a triptych, a boy's face smudged into the shadows. Hell
holds my eyes, the October afternoon a spectacle
of skin and decay.
                  Dead leaves. The gallery's post-lunch lull.
I am alone with three boy soldiers, screams stalled
mid gunfight, water gushing from pink muzzles.
I want to be part of this *Lol*,
a photon sailing towards the iPhone's lens, a syllable
of south Sahara's summer sound, their skulls'
golden skies.
             The Lord of War sells golden Kalashnikovs. Google
spews a despot's wiki page and a roll
of adverts morph into Bambi eyes, blue bottles
crawling cheeks dark as mine and bright as rot. I recall
my A-level years. Yugoslavia's white corpses. My cold smile.

Ishion Hutchinson
A Statue in Utopia

(Kingston)

Approach this city and remember Thebes,
overrun with priests; only here, thieves.
Cross-eyed, at the city's head, a minister
guards the ports, blood crusting his sceptre.

He never removes his spectacles; they screen
his eyes, two bloodshot stoves, shunting
in the heat. One of the blighted children
under his plaque charcoaled: "Friend..."

Men bay before him for alms and become rocks;
women bow breaking their heads in their laps.
His fly-gaze number them, slave labourers,
who never decline, and never too the robbers

routing in the minister's treasury and cabinet
where his rusty, grand riddles are still kept.
As sunset coppers the ports and slowly swarms
the sea, it claims his tireless, opened arms.

Sonnet L'Abbé
from Sonnet's Shakespeare:
154 Ecolonizations

V

Wealth. Rose hours, wealth. Create with gentleman's work the
diamond fraternity. Men, the all-over tally, gas and magazines,
wholly frère, forever, yes yes, of course. Do the odd good thing well.
We will play lithe servants and tall, striking tyrants. Toronto the
over-fleur-de-lys, and smaller men. Androcene isn't that unfair when
stitched up fairly, don't you authorize? Excellence forgets who nods,
never not arresting time. It leads. Sums america on the oh-so
ideologibeauteous. I win terabytes and Indo-companies founded on
ships of amaranth. Serotonin we sap, branches flecked with ferrous
tank-bled lusters. Why lead slaves quietly? Ego's nevers and beat and
duty move doers. Now dandies' bare branches kneel stillness
everywhere. Wealth, queens, other women, wren-mottled sums.
Home, ars discursia, stilled. Discrimination left and righted. Like
liquid enterprise owners spend to open satin walls of foreign alas, so
beauty sets affect. Win wealth, win beauty, wear red. Be referee to no
writing not porno or remembrance. What it was was nothing but
flowers. Distant ills are a hundredth, rough theory without winning
terms. Sonnet, let these butters sweeten the heir. Show them fair
resubstantialization of their finances. Till lives sweat, Sonnet.

Roger Robinson
Brixton Revo 2011

In caps, hoodies, bandannas, they streamed
through Brixton from small alleys armed with bottles,
scrap metal, bricks, smelling the petrol in the air,
the ashen taste of smoke on tongues,
they ransacked phone shops, darted in and out
of trainer shops lit by flares of fire and as thick black smoke
billowed from inside they stood still
for a few moments and surveyed their damage –
the crumpled iron shutters, jagged stalactites of glass

then, silently, the feral pack took off –

Kayo Chingonyi
from calling a spade a spade

The N Word

You came back as rubber lips, pepper grains, blik
you're so black you're blik and how the word stuck to
our tongues eclipsing – or so we thought – the fear
that any moment anyone might notice
and we'd be deemed the wrong side of a night sky.
Lately you are a *pretty little lightie* who can
get dark because – even now – dark means street
which means beast which means leave now for Benfleet.
These days I can't watch a music video
online without you trolling in the comments
dressed to kill in your new age binary clothes.

The Cricket Test

Picture a cricket match, first week at upper
school, blacks versus whites, that slight hesitation
on choosing a side, and you're close to knowing
why I've been trying to master this language.
Raised as I was, some words in this argot catch
in the throat, seemingly made for someone else
(the sticking point from which all else is fixed).
We lost to a one-handed catch. After the match
our changing room was a shrine to apartheid.
When I crossed the threshold, Danny asked me why
I'd stand here when I could be there, with my kind.

Anthony Joseph
Los Angeles Death Poem

Round about dirt roads to a dusty airport.
Hidden in the haze.
Waiting in the gully bush
to snap an axe.
Lawless in this red grove,
       ...waiting...

There is no difference between
this body and that.
There be no metal, no pulley,
no strange machine.
       Electric tissue of death.

Nick Makoha
The Republic

In 1979 when the world ends
there will be guns, AK-47s spitting
like mechanical dragonflies into a Kampala night.

There will be militia, who use barbed wire
like rope to hang men like cows
from the arms of trees by their genitals.

There will be melted corpses chewed
by hyenas at the roadside, even the stench
of urine will not curb their hunger.

The price of beer
will be cheaper than a loaf of bread
now that the Asians have gone.

Blood loosened by a machete blade
will flow down the Kisigi Hills
to the throat of Lake Victoria.

No longer will we fall
at Amin's feet as if dead,
even while the hills burn.

Jocelyn Page
In case of fire

Back burn.
This will stop the real flames
from gaining on you.
Choose the river
as your firebreak.
Bulldoze a clearing
to be safe.
Set ablaze
everything
in its path
that could feed it.

Then rest
in the knowledge
that someplace
in all that heat
natural and instigated
somewhere in the smoke
between winning and losing
there is a sequoia seed waiting
to crack and germinate in ash.

Caroline Smith
Selection

He was quietly hopeful
when he got the letter
that said his case had been
'selected for progression',
that he would be allowed to stay.
But then a second had arrived:
'an invitation to a service event'
and he was suspicious.
Too much activity –
this sudden attention to him.
He was scared.
It was as if after all these
years of hiding, he would,
finally be led out with the
other men and boys,
through the fringe of sunlight
from the gloom of the pine forest
his hands clasped behind his head.

Mir Mahfuz Ali
A Lizard by my Hospital Bed

The mouth of silence trickles forward a bloodless lizard.
I take off my oxygen mask and allow

his cracked sound to crawl into my teenage head.
Like me he puffs for air. I wheeze. He pants.

Does not break his meditation as the hours pass,
my eyes still on him when he jumps on a thinking fly

with a fine open-air gesture. An education by lizard:
focus, don't rely on impulse.

Keep the foam clear so my voice doesn't burst
through my trachea hole

like a grenade in a pomegranate.
My eyes flick a question, city kerosene-thuds

echoing in my head. My friend says nothing.
Goes one step back, two steps forward.

How can I let him go? I grab the fellow by his tail,
but he still escapes through the gap in my throat.

Ivy Alvarez
from The Everyday English Dictionary

D

detruncate:
> the lizard's tail wiggles
> long after the body has gone

deuterogamy:
> exchange rings
> old for new —
> fool her twice shame on her
> still the same bruise

devoir:
> of course one couldn't say this
> so the tongue is bit
> again and again

dewlap:
> the water buffalo is all muscle
> and would know no such thing

diacoustics:
> bent awkward 'round
> the corner of the room
> the sound of knuckles on bone

diaeresis:
> stretch the name to call them   back
>   forth   again
> bounces onto walls
> off into night

Diriye Osman
Watering the Imagination

While the boat people, those who are hungry for new homes in places like London and Luxembourg, risk their lives on cargo ships, I remain in Bosaaso. I tell stories to my daughter about warrior queens, freedom fighters, poets. Suldana is eighteeen. She spends her days working at our kiosk, selling milk and eggs; at night she sneaks out to the beach to see her lover. She crawls back into into bed at dawn, smelling of sea and salt and perfume. When she walks down the street, men stare and whistle and ache. They cannot have her. She is wrapped in a shawl of stars. Every day marriage proposals arrive with offers of high dowries. I wave them away. Many things go unsaid: how we love, who we love, why we love. I do not know why Suldana loves the way she does. I do know that I am letting her reach for something of which we cannot speak. Every evening we walk towards the water and write on scraps of paper. We tie the paper around stones using rubber bands. We fling the stones into the ocean. My mother and my mother's mother used to do this.

Suldana will sail forth from Somalia. She will not turn back.

سقي الخيال

Hannah Lowe
1918

after Ha Van Vuong, 'Boy with Bamboo'

I saw you on the gangplank Grandfather,
stood in the fevered sun with your chin raised up.

Nothing in this strange new world could faze you,
not the grave black faces on the dock,

the bone-thin men, the women in stained dresses;
not the rash-faced guards who read your papers,

their orders unfurling on pointed fingers, fingers
that gripped your wrists, and split open your mouth

to count your teeth. I saw you there, heaving
through the crush, searching out the voices

from the hold, small men with bright black hair,
sea-eyes like yours. And if I saw you there,

didn't I see you on the other side,
stepping through the silver daze of rain

on the Shanghai wharf with no-one behind you
waving goodbye, and nothing to go back to?

Didn't I see you, where the mountains puncture
the sky and the plains are cold and blue,

a river slicing through the troubled earth
where rusted shacks squat low. Didn't I see you,

peering through the reeds, small barefoot boy,
crouched down, with an armful of bamboo?

Moya Pacey
Port Vila

My father paints me white.
Stripes my shoulder
blades like feathers

circles my chest
my arms
ghost chains.

Places a manou
between my legs.
Follow me.

Grandfather shakes the clapping stick
feathers flapping.
Uncle beats the drum.

Father stamps his feet
I stamp
Father sings

I sing.

On the wharf you jingle coins;
clutch a can of coke
Father stops,

I stop.

You put a gold coin into his palm
Father says, *Thank you*
I say, *Thank you.*

You toss your empty coke can into our blue harbour.

POETRY PORTRAITS

Artist Yemisi Blake creates photographic responses to new poems by Elmi Ali and Jo Brandon

Elmi Ali
Made in Bangladesh

**Cotton hoodies show
that tides change and labour's never the same**

Jo Brandon
Bullen

It was my father's name – I bore my own and she hid from it

I wound that 'B' around my neck, stringing white, white pearls
they couldn't bruise, you couldn't bloody and whispered
to you in French, so my lacklustre truth couldn't translate
thickened in rich vowels: velvet against damp palms.
You translated my Latin through your masters
– who taught you only the words that please
smiled and held your gaze so you wouldn't get the wrong idea
too blanched to blush – you were red enough. Your changeable characters
let me write 'Sum A.B.' and you 'Fidelis pectus pectoris' that I lived
to believe. You never asked after our name. You remembered only one.
Sweetmeats fell from my dress, you let them fall devouring me instead
– 'modo niger et ustus fortiter', my swan song was not sweet
you let me keep a single gilded plume that they all recognise as me.

Bullen is an alternative spelling of the surname Boleyn

Hannah Lowe
Reggae Story

My father liked the blues and Lady Day.
He left Jamaica way before the reggae
rocked all night in backstreet studios,
before King Tubby or Augustus Pablo.
But I used to love a boy who loved
dub reggae, loved thick lugs of ganga, loved
on Sunday nights to cross the river, take me
to The House Of Roots and Aba-shanti
in the cobbled arches under Vauxhall
where the Lion of Judah decked the walls
and stacks of speakers pumped electric bass,
a single bulb above the smoky haze
and on the stage a little dreadlocked man
like Rumplestiltskin, shouted *Jah!* and span
his blistering tunes on a single turntable
and shut-eyed men called back over the vinyl
Jah, Selassie I. Next door, the old guys
were like wizened goats with yellow eyes
hunched over games of chess and ginger tea,
below the golden framed Haile Selassie,
king of kings. That boy didn't know my father
was a white-haired godless pensioner
and reggae music never really got me
until I played it on my own: Bob Marley,
U-Roy, Johnny Clark, and even then
it came like hymns or Faure's *Requiem*,
Vivaldi's *Gloria*. He thought I had
a Rasta like Prince Far-I for a dad
not the silent island man who sat
beyond the bedroom door I'd listen at
to catch a woman crooning down a melody:
I Can't Give You Anything, But Love, Baby

Edward Doegar
Half-Ghazal

for Reneé

> The word [Ghazal] is of Arabic origin and means 'talking to women'
> (women in purdah, with all that that implies).
> — Mimi Khalvati, Notes to The Meanest Flower

I flinch inside as you corroborate my name,
which is your name

now. You spell it out over the phone to a call centre
in India. Your new surname

as foreign to you as the phone-wallah
at the other end. Though the name

itself was born and bred in the Himalayas,
in Hindi, it's long been reformed into English, into the name

you now pronounce
in your own, non-native, North American. It's a name

you'll freely admit you'd rather not have taken
but have taken all the same, exchanging one unchosen name

for another, uncasting yourself as Kohanim.
And yes, I was proud you agreed bear to my name,

to belong to my skin,
to share the cloth of my sisters' maiden name.

But now, as you get used to an alias,
I recall my mother, who wouldn't disown her married name,

but lived with it, assimilated, as my father's
ex-wife, determined to keep the same last name

as me. You begin again: *Dee – Oh – Eee – Jee – Ay – Arr*
and I blush at the burden of our name.

Sophie Mayer
Londinos

Vote mice. Vote fox. Vote pellet, scuffle, track-stopping shadow.
Vote rosebay willowherb, mallow between paving stones, little mouse-ear,
dark mullein. Vote Walbrook, vote Fleet, vote Effra, vote for wet
pencil-traces on the map. Vote for Mother Red Cap, vote for Mother
Clap! Vote Boudicca, mark your cross for Boadicea, bring chariots of
Iceni fire. Vote Cornelius, lately come from Africa to sign his name
to the register of this parish, the year of our Lord 1593. A vote for Bevis
Marks and Princelet Street resounds the city's hills with the trumpet
of the Lord. Vote for a Durga Puja at the British
Museum, where Tagore once eyed the piratical
thievings. Vote Mary Read, roaring-boy hostage of Calico Jack.
Vote for Margery Jourdain: she can, or so they say, raise the dead. Vote down
Tyburn tree, vote down the Bailey, ersatz forest ripe with blasphemous
heads shouting treason, corruption, law's disorder.

Vote with a finger smirred with blackberries picked beneath the spriggan,
tongued patron saint of abandoned overground lines. Vote recumbent,
      like Oscar,
looking up, drunk, in hope of the stars. Graphite marks the hand
that marks the margins, overruns the boxes, poised for flight
when the light changes to green.

Londinos (Celtic): wild

Suzi Feay

The Masks

Hag of the Woods
Eyes like teacups, her lip
A chute for souls, old wagger,
Horsehead, Dreaming Hare
Red-rimmed with upgazing,
Inside Out, wearing her flayed flower.

Cream-Face, buttering sweetmeat
And balm. Paper-Skin
Fluttering her deft hands.
Sewn-Shut, so proper
Blindly tending her blooms.
Half-This-Half-That who cannot tell the truth,
Burnt-Face who cannot lie,
Old Sickle Moon rolling her dark house.
Hag of the Woods. Choose.

Rowyda Amin
Genius Loci

Rubbing my rhubarb in Washington Square, the infamous but
much-loved wearer of woolen hats in hot weather, the wonder
dog, lamper of gold-dust drudgers, champ of wild-goose pursuits,
I, the one man band, clockless animal, whistling Tarzan, crap in
the grass, rapture dalliance on benches, chuckle in my yellow
beard a fuzz of tasty syllables. My drinking glass, my hand
I raise to Bird Man, pigeons on his shoulders, blues harp in
his lips to acclaim the wide-mouthed tulips' velveteen wine
and Kool-Aid hues; to bronze Giuseppe's pill-box, sarcastic
squirrels mocking tourists from on top; but not those green
Visigoths, the singalongers peddling gods. I'll take real figs and
not their painted ones. And you, stoic lunch-hour zebra
bent at your tuna sandwich, shrink-wrapped in pinstriped
wool for the daily auto-da-fé: do you question that I am cobalt
to the blood, a rain charmer, frog prince for a nickel with
cocksure loll, human with the composition of smoke? I shoulder
the kiloton of cogitation, the torture of dayglo tigers padding
nonstop my yellow sleeps; but to any tethered chimp that
pities me my leper life, I proffer this garden cosmopolis,
its stores of salt and creamsicle, lucid dreamers with eyes wide.

Nicholas Laughlin
Reading History

The time was a page on which too much had been written,
in the racing hands of too many months and years.
Names of correspondents, station names,
dates of conversations, book reviews,
fragments of memoirs, directions to new hotels.
Mais que suis-je venu faire sur cette Terre?
And lives of pianists and architects and saints.
And the page was creased with too many hurried unfoldings.

And the houses grumbled with the weight of lists and pages.
The scent of lilies, the drawl of brief etudes.
It took longer to read about those months than to live them.
"It astonished me that my friends could be so forgiving."
"I was certain those meetings in April could never be repeated;
November proved me wrong." "I was surely lucky,
for S._____ had told no one else about my discovery."
"I was right." "It was there." "It had gone." "I was barely mistaken."

"We never read so much as we did on that visit.
We can have done nothing but read the entire week.
We walked in the afternoons, but even then
all we talked about was what we were reading."
A generation decided together in silence
to have done with fiction and to renounce the stage.
Nothing seemed lost. Everyone kept a diary.
Every remark or detail was preserved in their letters.

Three piano notes came drifting through the house
like yellow leaves, then the curtain swept them away.
No, they came like footsteps that hesitate,
or three pages that slowly turn in the evening draft.
He watched the pages turn and history begin.
Already many hands were crossing and tracing
in the steelpoint light of many jars of ink.
Three leaves fell, and already too much had been written.

Dzifa Benson
Coitus, Refracted

If something moves, then time is also bending.
It is stirring in the hidden shafts of hair follicles
standing on end, in the pliant opening of spine, disc by disc.

It makes space in the slinks and shifts of small caught breaths,
the in and the out of breast and chest. It stretches communion
in the dilation of a pupil, the rub of lips, the deepening thrust of hips.

To hold this rhythm of accord and live this exhaustion, to arrest
the gone of a moment in this petit mort of limbs, we become all
things that move – lava, waterfall, glacier, the wind, a pulse.

Sex returns us to what science can't measure, a big bang
beginning time, light passing through our bodies and, we moan.

Sophie Clarke
Internet Dating

Too timid to meet, we
never met. I fell in love

with reams of bandwidth, impossible
as the bright scarves streaming
from a magician's mouth, with ribbons
of cable, exquisite pixels, sequined.
With your Comic Sans, which I ate up
like dark seeds, or
my face bathed in blue
at one o'clock in the morning, that
pale light which made me beautiful.

And I thought we might break
into song, like nineteen-eighties star-
crossed lovers, like the young couple
on match.com, but your shy vowels
only crackled over the mic, my voice
amplified, quite unlike my own,
and suddenly we were both

ourselves and not. That night
I snapped my laptop shut
as dawn broke yellow
as a yolk into glass
over blackened moors.
Solid. Astoundingly
physical.

Matthew Gregory
A Room in Taiwan, 2010

And how many desert miles of the web
    has she crossed tonight searching
for the home address of Mastroianni.

Mastroianni is no longer among us.
    She does not know this so continues
her drift from one ruined domain

to the next one, signing herself in
    to empty guestbooks as she goes.
I would like to write to Mr Marcello Mastroianni

please if anyone know where he is.
    I dream us in light of stars and great city Rome.
I want to be like kiss of Anita Ekberg.

Mastroianni whose thousand pictures
    in these forums lose him on pages
like palimpsests of man on top of man

where this girl, at her tropical desk,
    who lists for his deep, romantic heart
touches a hit-counter, once, in the dark.

Brigid Rose
The World is Made of Paper

> *Form is emptiness, emptiness is form.*
> – Ancient Buddhist Sutra

It is paper – reams of the flimsiest gift-wrap
with a plain, repeated pattern.
In a world so weakly, it doesn't take much;
with your bare hands, you can rip it apart.

You step out, poke your fingers through walls,
pull up pavements, punch holes in pitches, courts, lawns.
You crash through bank vaults, through prison cell bars,
crush cars in your palms, tear down shops, houses, great aged halls.

With your bare hands, you can rip apart the world.

You know this destruction makes you unlovely
but you don't stop. A frenzied Shiva – all arms and hands,
laughing as you go, you rid the world of everything unsatisfactory
and satisfactory also.

You lay waste to whole streets, do away
with industries, networks of roads.
You demolish villages, abolish towns,
eradicate landscapes, eliminate coasts, nations, realms.

With your bare hands, you tear the world to shreds.

And when every last thing to be torn is tattered,
you relent. You take a breath, blow away the mess,
find this ripping has unleashed not hell,
but an inadvertent heaven.

The unwrapped world is this:
a glorious nothing, an unsought present.
There is no home to return to.
You house yourself utterly in emptiness.

Ishion Hutchinson
Home Sea

Portland, land-of-ports, ubiquitous sea,
bay of missionaries, where forts with rusted
cannons still await the bugle of empire.

Occasionally, in Port Antonio, a cruise ship
dots the bay, or a rich European's yacht,
and for a brief while, white ghosts

haunt the marina's restaurant, Coronation market,
and like marlins, break the water
at San San, at Winnefred, at Bryan's Bay.

Every spray of seawater is history.

The blond boy diving, comes up to see
the straw hat lifeguard, worried like hell, watching.
The guard watches, overseer of water,

a babysitter to a baby that this morning
ate ackee, and said, in the presence
of the serving lady, "This shit is good as gold."

In that philosophy is all of history.

The boy ate El Dorado's ackee; shat
himself and now swims, full-bellied, in the piratical
patch of pure blue. Once, an Indian boy

from St. Thomas had gone swimming
after eating ackee. They called him Fishhead,
a lithe boy, eel body, true swimmerman.
He drowned. It was the ackee, three heads grieving

in a pod. The blond boy dips under again.

EPILOGUE

❧

Geraldine Clarkson
flotsam

ghostcraft
nudges Uncle Sam:
anniversary

***

from longitude one three eight
latitude three six:
magnitude nine

***

fragments   fragments
garments   garments

remnants   remnants

***

crumpledcrumbledrocked

***

rem levels rising
riding the curl
random planks

***

hot iodine
cold shutdown reactors
child's torn shout

***

survivors live with fear
survivors live

***

tsunamiflotsami

***

a few old shoes, some blankets,
boy's toy car; brand-new
orphans

Otsuchi, they are gone now, the cowled sea-monk is leading them through fronded corridors and milky halls mother-of-pearl panelled, limpet floor-lit. A cleaner fish is purging them of all that was judged crusty – where the rush of blood dried and unbeautiful things bruised the future. Coral tables creak under sea cucumbers, gooseberries, and crabs loading cardamom carapaces with fat anemones

***

Fukushima peaches
pretty deadly
avoid gutters and shrubs
which suck in sickness

***

Thongs of knotted wrack hold back eager water-curtains while watchful sturgeon and flagellant gulls peek and peck. Swells like coughs and cuffs from a playing whale nudge them forward, pull and roil. A shellbell calls them all to Compline

Out of the depths I have cried –
rads –
rubbish –

Hold back, Otsuchi, it's no use your forking left and right won't prosper you now. A handful of hours, at most, and they'll be home and dry

***

twisted ship
rusty remembrance
one Spring on

Note: One year on from the March 2011 Japanese tsunami, a drifting 'ghost ship' approached the coast of the USA, and was later sunk by the US Coast Guard.

CENTREFOLD

ℬ

When I was a sculptor I'd been involved in the feminist movement in the visual arts and believed that women artists had something different to bring to the canon. We were not just genderless people who only had the option of copying what men had done.

– *Pascale Petit*

Do Women Poets Write Differently To Men?

PASCALE PETIT

Two years ago I took part in a discussion at the Aldeburgh Poetry Festival called 'The Female Poem'. Jo Shapcott, Annie Freud, Maureen Duffy and I considered the question: do women write different poems from men and, if so, what could be said to characterise the 'female' poem? It was nine on a Sunday morning and the hall was packed, with men as well as women. The event sold out within minutes of being advertised and had to be moved to a larger venue, which suggests the subject is pressing.

We considered whether it might be more useful to think in terms of 'feminine' and 'masculine' poetry, rather than the division of gender, and that some men might write feminine poems and some women masculine poems. Jo said that when writing *Of Mutability* she was intrigued by the idea of art that might not declare gender. She also pointed out that "the idea of identifying the female poem may then push one outside a bit further, because we don't talk about the male poem in quite the same way; it's as if the male poem is the default".

We agreed that this idea of the woman poet as outsider could have its advantages. I said that being on the margins might give women a clearer vision, and that there are women poets who write strange poetry, creating haunting and distinct worlds. Emily Dickinson is one example:

> As all the Heavens were a Bell,
> And Being, but an Ear,
> And I, and Silence, some strange Race
> Wrecked, solitary, here –
>
> And then a Plank in Reason, broke,
> And I dropped down, and down –   ('I felt a Funeral, in my Brain')

Other examples include Selima Hill, Medbh McGuckian, Moniza Alvi, Pauline Stainer, Charlotte Mew and, internationally, Valérie Rouzeau, Alfonsina Storni, Doris Kareva and Zhai Yongming. The strangeness may come from women's marginal position as well as their closer relationship with the body, and its wonder, shock and messiness. Here is McGuckian on the Incarnation:

> We will have to understand some such
> word as 'today', a luminous Word
> for the 'until' verse of the god-
> making, brief Messianic stir
> air-kissing the harmony of the data
>
>   ('Chairé')[1]

The sequence this is taken from explores the Incarnation, but it can equally be read as a study of how astonishing it is for a human life to begin inside a person. Similarly, Moniza Alvi's poem 'Mermaid' displays an unease with the body, female sexuality symbolised by a fishtail which is invaded by a man:

> She danced an involuntary dance
> captive
>   twitching with fear.
>
> Swiftly
>   he slit
>
> down the muscular length
> exposing the bone in its red canal.   ('Mermaid')[2]

    The strange quality of some women's poetry reminds me of women surrealist painters. Artists such as Remedios Varo, Leonora Carrington, Frida Kahlo, and, later on, Annette Messager, Tabitha Vevers and Louise Bourgeois, differ from their male counterparts in that they are depicting a woman's hitherto unmapped imagination, which can reveal an alternative world to the default male one. Remedios Varo painted spiritual other-worlds but Frida Kahlo, according to Diego Rivera, was: "the only example in the history of art of an artist who tore open her chest and heart to reveal the biological truth of her feelings". In Kahlo's case the body dominates her imagery. But is a poem by a woman different to a man's if the main focus of the work is not the body?

---

1. *The Book of the Angel*, Gallery Books, 2004.
2. *Europa*, Bloodaxe Books, 2008.

Or, to turn the argument on its head: are there features of men's poems that mark them out as made by men? Of course there are male poets who write strange poetry – Rilke is supremely otherworldly – but (hard as it is to generalise) men's strangeness might be more in relation to the centre, rather than the margins. Peter Redgrove, who has been described by Seamus Heaney as "a conjurer of strangeness", could be viewed as a more 'feminine' poet, although his poems pulse with electro-erotic currents that have a masculine energy.

Don Paterson, reviewing Les Murray's *Collected Poems* in the summer 1992 issue of *Poetry Review*, praised Murray's sprawl and range, implying that these are masculine attributes: "Les Murray writes big poems. Big, fat, long, hairy-arsed, man-sized poems. Poems that stretch as far as the eye can see, like one of those Australian sheep-farms the size of Wales." This comment made a lasting impression on me, as I was still developing as a poet then and Murray was (and still is) one of my favourite poets. There were not so many women poets I could turn to as role models in the eighties and early nineties, but Murray, with his emphasis on the trance aspect of writing, his extraordinary ability to identify with creatures from the natural world, and his disregard of fashions, was an exemplar. But here was a male reviewer speaking to other men about Murray's male virtues as a poet; though Murray, with his extreme sensitivity and empathy with his non-human subjects, seems to have as many feminine as masculine characteristics in his writing (assuming that empathy as a trait is more feminine than masculine!).

Conversely, the sprawl that Paterson praises, though perhaps unique to Murray, might be a quality to which some female poets aspire, even though historically one of the criticisms levelled at them is a tendency to narrowness of scope, limiting verse to the domestic sphere. This apparent narrowness is not just a criticism confined to Britain. At this year's London Book Fair I asked the Chinese poet and critic Xi Chuan what he thought of women's poetry in China, because during visits there I was struck by how reserved women poets were. In Xi Chuan's memorable response, he said that "women poets write like a flame", and that he "can tell it's a poem written by a woman with the first line". He admitted that they are not as well known as men, but thought they are better poets, though tend to write on less big themes. He added that although their reach is narrower, often limited to the home, their subjects are not less important.

Yet as early as 1900, the Qing Dynasty poet Qiu Jin wrote:

Don't tell me women
are not the stuff of heroes,
I alone rode over the East Sea's
winds for ten thousand leagues.
My poetic thoughts ever expand,
like a sail between ocean and heaven.
My poetic imagination ranges far and wide,
as freely as a sailboat on an open sea...

('Capping Rhymes with Sir Shih Ching From Sun's Root Land')[3]

I cite the case of Chinese poetry because it is an explicit example of the suppression of female poetry in a culture, whereas in the UK the suppression was covert. As Michelle Yeh wrote, in her introduction to her *Anthology of Modern Chinese Poetry*: "Just as women have been traditionally marginalized in Chinese society [...] so, too, have women poets occupied a peripheral place in the literary canon, the range of their poetry bound by literary conventions and moral constraints narrower and more rigid than those for men". The Chinese situation has since improved, especially with the advent of the contemporary feminist poet Zhai Yongming, and her concept of "Black Night consciousness" – the otherness or darkness of female poetry.

But are women's themes restricted in British and Irish poetry? As I ponder that question I keep turning to Eavan Boland's poignant book, *A Journey with Two Maps: Becoming a Woman Poet* (Carcanet, 2011), where she describes the courage it took for her to write about domestic life after the birth of her first child, against the Irish tradition of male rhetoric. Her argument is that the domestic is no less important than the streets of Irish history. In the chapter 'Letter to a Young Woman Poet' she says:

> But the past I want to talk about is more charged and less lyrical than that for women poets. It is, after all, the place where authorship of the poem eluded us. Where poetry itself was defined by and in our absence [...] But there is also a difficult and dangerous walking on ice, as we try to find language and images for a consciousness we are just coming into and with little in the past to support us.

This makes me consider my own journey, and how sparse the vista was

---

3. Translated by Zachary Jean Chartkoff.

when I looked for influences. When I was a sculptor I'd been involved in the feminist movement in the visual arts and believed that women artists had something different to bring to the canon. We were not just genderless people who only had the option of copying what men had done. When I stopped making sculptures to concentrate on writing poetry, again I struggled to find role models. I revered Sylvia Plath, not for her life story but her way with language, though it was impossible to imitate her. I scoured the first women's anthologies for guidance, but *One Foot on the Mountain: Anthology of British Feminist Poetry* (Onlywomen Press, 1979) and *Bread and Roses* (Virago, 1982) seemed to be more about making a stand against the patriarchal tradition, rather than creating powerful alternatives. Much of the poetry explored women's subjects, such as giving birth, which, although groundbreaking, was also limiting.

Jeni Couzyn's *Bloodaxe Book of Contemporary Women Poets* (1985) was the first in a string of women's anthologies from Bloodaxe, the publisher which went on "to transform the publishing opportunities for women poets, not because they are women poets but because they are outstanding writers by any standard [...] Bloodaxe has been unusual in having a poetry list which is 50:50 male: female."[4]

Then in 1993, *The Virago Book of Birth Poetry* also included poems by men. The introduction by Charlotte Otten was encouraging; she described Anne Sexton breaking the taboo of women's subjects with her poem 'In Praise of My Uterus': "Sexton caused an earthquake. The male world lost its equilibrium; the female world burst into poetry. Women's bodies became the poetry. No aspect of pregnancy was considered too embarrassing, too trivial, or too private for a poem."

These were milestones, but I still looked for the wide horizons described by Qiu Jin, wanted my imagination to wander "far and wide", specifically to the Amazonian wilderness which I'd visited. My main influences at that time were still male poets, until I discovered Sharon Olds and Selima Hill. I admired Olds's directness, but was as impressed by her syntax and the way she wove metaphoric images into her narratives as I was with her themes. Hill seemed to be doing something highly original and at the same time female. Again, the themes were gripping, but it was her proliferation of surreal images that felt expansive. They have a "sprawl" – her poems are a freshly shaken world:

---

4. Neil Astley, *In Person: 30 Poets* (Bloodaxe Books, 2008).

I left the room,
and slipped into the garden,
where I gulped down whole mouthfuls of delicious aeroplanes
that taxied down my throat
still wrapped in sky
with rows of naked women in their bellies...   ('Why I Left You')[5]

Hill is an example of an 'outsider' sensibility, but the profusion of women poets who have emerged in the last decade offers an array of possibilities. There are women who write like men, who engage with the tradition on its own terms, and there are those who are re-inventing that tradition. Alice Oswald is an example of a poet who engages fully with the tradition, but also re-invents it. Recent single-sex anthologies such as *Modern Women Poets* and *Women's Work* display the confidence and sheer range of women's writing but the real breakthrough is in mixed anthologies where men do not dominate the gender ratio, as in Salt's *The Best British Poetry* series. Also, *Ten: New Poets from Spread the Word* (Bloodaxe Books, 2010), which features seven women poets and three men, indicates that in the future, women-only anthologies might become unnecessary.

In *Ten*, Karen McCarthy Woolf fuses female themes, such as losing a baby, with an ambitious playfulness with form. In the highly kinetic 'Mor Bleu', inspired by Anselm Kiefer's installation *Palm Sunday*, a collage of voices cascades through the air. This is poetry that is as formally exciting as it is emotional:

> — we haven't got —
>   a heart   beat
>   — haven't got five minutes
> a groan of sea
>   shushes up on shore
>
>   — rushes and there's no —
> no *ha ha ha* of music

Like McCarthy Woolf, who draws on an English/Jamaican heritage, Malika Booker delves into the rich tradition of her Guyanese background to bring us tales from beyond these shores, as in 'Pepper Sauce':

5. *Violet*, Bloodaxe Books, 1997)

I hear she scoop up that pepper sauce out of an enamel bowl,
and pack it deep into she granddaughter pussy,
I hear there was one piece of screaming in the house that day...

There is a rawness in such writing that feels fresh, yet it is as lyrical as it is terrifying. The increasing visibility of women poets with multicultural roots further invigorates the picture. Ultimately, the answer to the question: "do women poets write differently to men" for me is yes, but I acknowledge that, for many, gender is not relevant to their craft, and welcome the plurality of approaches. The variety is thrilling and open-ended.

Pascale Petit's fifth collection *What the Water Gave Me: Poems after Frida Kahlo* was shortlisted for both the T.S. Eliot Prize and Wales Book of the Year, and was a book of the year in the *Observer*.

ℬ

The judges of the Ted Hughes Award for New Work in Poetry 2012, **Maura Dooley**, **Ian Duhig** and **Cornelia Parker**, are currently accepting recommendations from Poetry Society and Poetry Book Society members.

Eligible works include, but are not limited to: poetry collections (for adults or children), individual published poems, radio poems, verse translations, verse dramas, verse novels, libretti, film poems and poetry in public art.

Recommendations for the 2012 award will be accepted until 4 January 2013. Download a form from www.poetrysociety.org.uk

TED HUGHES
AWARD FOR
NEW WORK
IN POETRY

THE
POETRY
SOCIETY

www.poetrysociety.org.uk

Indian Poetry: An Experimental Continuity

RANJIT HOSKOTE

The spectre of authenticity has long haunted every discussion of the arts and culture in postcolonial India. This is understandable when viewed against the backdrop of the nationalist struggle for independence from the British Empire, during which ideology rather than historical accuracy became the touchstone for aesthetic judgement. From the eighteen nineties onward, an emergent class of largely Anglophone Indian intellectuals translated the antagonisms of the political domain into the cultural sphere, scrutinising every form of expression for the degree to which it was 'indigenous' or 'alien', 'native' or 'derivative'. Ironically, the idea of an authentic 'Indianness' was all too often the expression of a deeply internalised auto-Orientalism: the acceptance by Indians, as a true mirror image, of the notion of India's cultural essence as defined and interpreted by a concourse of European scholars and cultural activists including William Jones, Monier Williams, Max Mueller, E.B. Havell and Ananda Kentish Coomaraswamy. Heavily classical in its emphasis, such an idea of India's cultural essence relied mainly on Hindu paradigms of religious experience and Sanskrit philosophical sources. This essence, it was implied, was resilient enough to survive several millennia of foreign invasion and domination, and would outlast the British Empire as well.

While this idea of an eternal India played its role in inspiring the popular resistance against British rule, which culminated in India's independence in 1947, it completely denies the actual history of transcultural encounters, stretching across three millennia, from which the complex artistic and cultural tapestry of India has been woven. Every such encounter has produced vibrant results; while the memories of conquest and oppression have passed into folklore, the concrete results of technological and cultural dialogue have passed into everyday life, in the form of language, imagery, narrative and ritual. India's encounter with Graeco-Roman culture in the first and second centuries CE produced, for the first time in history, a human image for the Buddha, among other iconographic innovations. Similarly, India's encounter with Islam between the eleventh and thirteenth centuries created a new language, Urdu, as well as new forms of Sufi and Bhakti devotionalism. In the same vein, India's colonial encounter with Europe threw up a series of new interfaces between oral or scribal literary traditions and print modernity, a feudal world-view premised on the infallibility of kingship, and the Enlightenment discourse of reason and the dignity of the individual, and, eventually, between Indian models of poetics and the dazzling experiments of artistic modernism.

Contemporary Indian poetry originates in these historic moments of tension and transition, especially as they were dramatised in the public debates of the late nineteenth and early twentieth centuries among such figures as Havell and Coomaraswamy, who have already been mentioned, as well as Rabindranath Tagore and Mahatma Gandhi, all of whom were advocates for various schools of cultural politics as well as literary practitioners. Among the key themes and questions thrown up by these debates were these: Was the citizen of a liberated India to be a bearer of a retrieved, largely re-imagined tradition, or was s/he to be the beneficiary of the Enlightenment? How would the new Indian subjectivity resolve the perceived contradiction between the traditional and spiritually oriented understanding of culture and the secularisation of experience through the processes of modernity? Were Indian writers to serve as the voices of literary genealogies sunk from view, or could they shake off this ideologically imposed burden and align themselves with Yeats, Pound, Eliot, Wallace Stevens and others in an international community of modernists, who would overturn and recalibrate the instruments of poetry?

In the history of Anglophone poetry in India, in particular, we find these dilemmas of national identity, cultural location and artistic choice being confronted and negotiated in diverse ways, through numerous generations of practitioners beginning with Henry Derozio (despite his name and Eurasian origins, an early Indian cultural nationalist) and his circle in the Calcutta of the eighteen twenties and continuing into the present, through the writings and discussions of poets both at home and in the Indian diaspora. Anglophone Indian poets are often productively Janus-faced: as inheritors of multiple cultural lineages and literary contexts, they operate in a threshold condition of rich hybridity even while having to defend themselves against charges of inauthenticity, dislocation, and unrootedness. The specific predicament of the Anglophone Indian poet begins with her or his choice of language. Nativist critics have typically regarded this as evidence of a desire to deny the claims of the nation (always constructed and imagined as somehow 'pre-English', especially by nativists who write in English) and to belong in an international ecumene; however, the fact is that

English is no longer a deliberate linguistic choice for many Indians, so much as it is a historical and sociological given. As the poet, fiction writer and translator Dilip Chitre (1938-2009) wrote:

> Indian English poets operate inside an alien linguistic space, the space of Indian languages... [Theirs] is the poetry of a landless minority and not an outpost of a dominant world literary culture... A sense of exile has to be an irreducible part of the Indian English poet's self-perception. He is therefore forced into an inner territory or a surrogate landscape as a substitute for a linguistic homeland. This is not a bleak prospect in itself. On the contrary, it is exciting and rich in potential.[1]

What nativist criticism wilfully chooses to ignore is the refusal of Anglophone Indian poetry to confine itself to banal and conscriptive dogmas of cultural selfhood. It is the legatee, not of the nation, but of modernism – which, far from being a purely European invention, was a laboratory of transcultural encounters with the art of India, China, Nigeria and Persia. Ezra Pound's radical poetics of imagism was nourished, we must remember, by his discovery of the compressed, elliptical measures of T'ang poetry in Arthur Waley's translation. Similarly, Jacob Epstein's figurative sculpture was transformed through his conversations with Coomaraswamy on Mauryan and Gupta sculpture, and Matisse and Picasso's understanding of the iconic potential of the human figure was dramatically influenced by their viewing of the Benin bronzes.

In this transgressive, transcultural spirit, Anglophone Indian poetry crafts its images and narratives from diverse cultural materials, splicing experiences from widely separated psychological domains, re-tuning inherited aesthetic models to carry the thrum of the contemporary. In the work of poets such as Nissim Ezekiel, A.K. Ramanujan, Adil Jussawalla, Dilip Chitre, Arvind Krishna Mehrotra, Keki N. Daruwalla, Agha Shahid Ali, Tabish Khair, Rukmini Bhaya Nair and Jeet Thayil, we find vibrant, complex, scintillating adaptations and transferences taking place between several Indian aesthetic idioms (ranging from the formal cadences of Sanskrit and Old Tamil to the more relaxed forms of Bhakti devotional poetry) and the idioms associated with Yeats, Auden, the surrealists, or the Black Mountain poets.

The poet, translator and cultural anthropologist A.K. Ramanujan

---

1. Dilip Chitre, 'Vague Targets: Some Thoughts on Indian English Poetry and (of course) Poetry in General', *The Bombay Literary Review* (No: 1, 1991), p. 32.

(1929-1993), for instance, often carried the spirit and tonality of the great Tamil anthologies of the early centuries CE into the present, and into the contours of English. He addresses the ancient Dravidian god of youth and joy in 'Prayers to Lord Murugan', a hymn that oscillates between the ironic and the melancholy, robust common sense and a transcendental awareness:

> Lord of headlines,
> help us read
> the small print.
>
> Lord of the sixth sense,
> give us back
> our five senses.
>
> Lord of solutions,
> teach us to dissolve
> and not to drown.[2]

Arvind Krishna Mehrotra (born 1947), poet, essayist and translator of the saint-poet Kabir, often infuses his own poetry with the spiritual master's pithy wisdom, earthy wit and awareness of the transience of all created things, combining it with the fruits of his long apprenticeship to Surrealism in poetry and the cinema, his fascination with the enigmatic revelations of hypnosis and dream. In 'Where Will the Next One Come From', he writes:

> The next one will come from the air
> It will be an overripe pumpkin
> It will be the missing shoe
>
> The next one will climb down
> From the tree
> When I'm asleep
>
> The next one I will have to sow
> For the next one I will have
> To walk in the rain
>
> The next one I shall not write
> It will rise like bread
> It will be the curse coming home[3]

2. A.K. Ramanujan, *Selected Poems* (New Delhi: Oxford University Press, 1976), p. 55.
3. Arvind Krishna Mehrotra, *Middle Earth* (New Delhi: Oxford University Press, 1984), p. 31.

The barriers of space and time dissolve in the politically nuanced, aesthetically complex poetry of Agha Shahid Ali (1949-2001); they are replaced by the threads of dialogues, through which the poem addresses crises that seem to have no resolution, which summon forth compassion while holding resolution at bay. In 'Ghazal', Ali conducts a conversation with several poets, traverses minefields and militarised zones: he invokes the memory of Federico Garcia Lorca, the Andalusian poet and playwright who revived the memory of Islamic Spain's vibrant culture through his art and was murdered by fascists; he addresses the Israeli poet Yehuda Amichai over the tragedy of Palestine. Ali achieves all this using the ghazal, a traditional form in Urdu poetry in which a series of couplets are strung together into a garland, unified by the repeated word that ends every alternate line. 'Ghazal' reads, in part:

> When Lorca died, they left the balconies open and saw:
> His *qasidas* braided, on the horizon, into knots of Arabic.
>
> Memory is no longer confused, it has a homeland—
> Says Shammas: Territorialize each confusion in a graceful Arabic.
>
> Where there were homes in Deir Yassein, you'll see dense forests—
> That village was razed. There's no sign of Arabic.
>
> I too, O Amichai, saw the dresses of beautiful women.
> And everything else, just like you, in Death, Hebrew, and Arabic.
>
> They ask me to tell them what *Shahid* means—
> Listen: It means 'The Beloved' in Persian, 'witness' in Arabic.[4]

From the early nineteen nineties onward, a new generation of Anglophone Indian poets has marked their departure from the themes and questions that haunted their predecessors. At home in a world in which the boundary between the local and the global has been increasingly blurred, they wrestle, in their poetry, with the ethical and artistic dilemmas produced by such a blurring. They live in India's major cities or are part of the South Asian diaspora; their poetry reflects the formal assurance and urbane fluency of their metropolitan location. They are keenly responsive to their crisis-

---

4. Agha Shahid Ali, *The Country Without A Post Office: Poems 1991-1995* (New Delhi: Ravi Dayal, 2000), pp. 47-48.

ridden lifeworld: a political environment menaced by violence, repression, and mounting emergency; an economy dominated by global capital and threatened by its vagaries; a society churned by the continuing struggle between elite and subaltern constituencies. This generation of poets is not even remotely apologetic about writing in English; they feel no obligation to prove their Indianness to nativist detractors. While most of them are polyglot, English is the language they inhabit, reshape and extend more than they do any other.

If the poetry of this generation springs from a metropolitan consciousness informed by the experiences of speed, isolation and catastrophe, it can also overcome the brittleness of the contemporary to adapt, critically, the forms and impulses of multiple traditions. Experiments with the villanelle and the sonnet coexist with attempts to conduct into English the silhouettes of the ghazal and the *doha*. And if these poets sometimes vein their work with a nostalgia for the forfeited homelands and archives of belonging, they also delight in improvising new forms of dialogue addressing an audience that changes form and definition constantly. As Jeet Thayil (born 1959) records his position, in the defiantly titled poem, 'English':

> and I would be ruined still by syntax, the risk
> and worry of committing word to stone.
> English fills my right hand, silence my left.[5]

Tabish Khair (born 1966), reflecting on poetic models lost during the passage through colonialism to modernity and found again in chance asides, memorialises such a rediscovery in 'The Other Half of Kabir's Doha', recalling:

> The time I voiced a line from your dohas, Kabir,
> Struggling to set it free from the prison of a book,
> And heard my grandfather's wordless cook
> Casually complete your couplet.[6]

Capturing the high ground of Sanskrit scholarship from its patriarchal, Brahminical guardians, the poet and theorist Rukmini Bhaya Nair (born 1952) uses the unpunctuated style of the Sanskrit *sloka* or aphorism in 'Genderole'; the vigour of its feminist argument explodes as we add the punctuation

---

5. Jeet Thayil, *English* (New Delhi: Penguin, 2003), p. 39.
6. Tabish Khair, in Ranjit Hoskote ed., *Reasons for Belonging: Fourteen Contemporary Indian Poets* (New Delhi: Penguin/ Viking, 2002), p. 24.

ourselves, deciphering this poem, one elegantly ferocious phrase at a time:

> Itmaybebeneathyoutopriseapartthisgimmick
> Butremembertheethingawomanchangesbestishersex
> [...]
> Muchhardertoconvertourselveshaving
> Labouredlongatbeingmenwepossessnothing[7]

If these poets claim affinity with Agha Shahid Ali, Arvind Krishna Mehrotra and Adil Jussawalla, they have also crafted a genealogy for themselves from an eclectic and global range of exemplars and reference figures, including Wallace Stevens and Hart Crane, Osip Mandelstam and Miguel Hernández, Charles Simic and Jorie Graham, Adrienne Rich and James Merrill, Tu Fu and Li Po. This generation of poets has benefited from the paradoxes of globalisation, a process that enslaves economies and condemns millions to the rigours of forced migration and alienated labour, but can also dissolve borders, enable the creation of unpredictable networks of exchange and liberate the imagination in unexpected ways.

Ranjit Hoskote is a poet, cultural theorist and curator. He is the Editor of *Dom Morales: Selected Poems* (Penguin Modern Classics, 2012).

ℬ

Select Bibliography
Amit Chaudhuri, *Clearing A Space: Reflections on India, Literature and Culture* (New Delhi: Permanent Black, 2008).
Ranjit Hoskote, ed., *Reasons for Belonging: Fourteen Contemporary Indian Poets* (New Delhi: Penguin/ Viking, 2002).
Sudeep Sen ed., *The HarperCollins Book of English Poetry* (New Delhi: HarperCollins, 2012).
Jeet Thayil ed., *The Bloodaxe Book of Contemporary Indian Poets* (Tarset: Bloodaxe Books, 2008).

7. Rukmini Bhaya Nair, in Jeet Thayil ed., *The Bloodaxe Book of Contemporary Indian Poets* (Tarset: Bloodaxe Books, 2008), p. 252.

Queer Poetry By Definition

CHERRY SMYTH

The word 'queer' was grasped as a proud thistle in the nineteen eighties largely in response to the homophobia and indifference to the HIV/ AIDS emergency; and as a rallying cry against Clause 28, a British law that made it illegal to discuss (ie 'promote') homosexuality in schools or publicly-funded groups. It eschewed the positive imagery campaigns that attempted to make gay and lesbian 'lifestyles' more acceptable to the hetero mainstream, and developed a strategy that was unapologetic, sexual and raging. Its sexually bold aesthetic welcomed anyone who renounced the privileges of heteronormativity and was willing to call themselves queer regardless of their sexual object choice. It created a cultural and activist explosion: a giant, liberating wave of energised belonging led by artists and writers such as Karen Finley, Essex Hemphill, Derek Jarman and Eileen Myles.

Queer poetry strived to define itself differently from lesbian and gay poetry in its politics, linguistics, address and audience. As Amy King explains in 'The What Else of Queer Poetry': "A queer poetry is the province to surpass identity... to open to the other scary self I think I am not and find another way to be." Queer promised a way to inhabit shame as well as 'gay pride' and re-eroticise the lesbian and gay body. In her scintillating essay, 'Hanging Out Beneath Orlando's Oak Tree, or Towards a Queer British Poetry', Sophie Mayer puts it: "To be queer is to look with new-fangled eyes at the body"and indeed proclaim it as a site of politicised experience.

More than twenty years later, the definition between gay and lesbian, and queer, has blurred and the category of queer gained a different kind of fluidity. By the nineteen nineties when queer had become assimilated to market white gay male culture and commodities, the term LGBT (lesbian, gay, bisexual, transgender) became a common shorthand, one that I suspect makes it easier for heterosexuals to avoid uttering the word 'lesbian', but a term that tries for more inclusivity. Mayer suggests that queer remains a radical tool in the US. While poets, she argues, were intrinsic to liberation struggles like the Civil Rights Movement in the States, poetry in Britain is embedded in the establishment. She bemoans the lack of sexual explicitness in British poetry, saying, "We're here, we're queer – but that here is circumscribed, crypto-queer in code and wink" and argues convincingly that queer visibility is hijacked by "the subtle censorship of sexuality, the coy refusal of pronouns, the curtailing of inappropriate emotions, the implicit suppression of political speech". A queer poet laureate? I don't think so.

So what is queer poetry? Is it defined by same-sex object choice, by self-appellation, by its reader, its LGBT themes, its confrontational erotics and/or its language and aesthetics? Queer poets have long sought out alternative venues such as clubs, galleries and festivals, and circulated their work through zines, chapbooks, and online and print-on-demand outlets, sustaining a vibrant, if poor, subculture. *Chroma Magazine*, edited by Shaun Levin and various poetry editors, 2004-10, published new and known queer writers and poets, and ran a successful queer poetry competition. But does publication by a more mainstream poetry press signal a dilution of the queer sensibility of protest? Can frankness be expressed without sexual explicitness?

What is striking about Maitreyabandhu's first pamphlet, *The Bond*, 2011, is the sequence of poems about his gay relationship from the age of eight to sixteen years with a boy called Stephen. Maitreyabandhu sets up the coded illicitness of an ongoing queer encounter that had to remain secret against the nascent sexual desire of the child and teenager he was. In 'The Dam', Maitreyabandhu exploits the pastoral lyric tradition of the mill, the brook, "the leaning trees" to lead the reader softly towards the hiding place where the boys "spread our coats out on the ground". The fearful shame is brilliantly evoked by the line: "(I never took the dogs; I couldn't bear / for them to watch.)", while in 'The Name' (forthcoming in *The Crumb Road*) the boys seem to become meek and tender animals. The adult narrator says that he cannot remember the nasty name he called Stephen, the name he was chased and hit for calling, but he does remember "you / climbing up the kitchen stairs, naked / on your hands and knees, and me following." I hardly know which words are more shocking: "kitchen stairs on your hands and knees" or "naked". The narrator has named himself.

The guilt that poetry helps us to write our way out of is also present in Jay Bernard's work. In 'Punishment' (*English Breakfast*, 2011) Bernard writes about the time her mother found her diary and read that her daughter had called her a bitch.

> 'Since you are so big,' she said, shaking the diary,
> 'let me remind you that it is my pussy you came from.'

The mother then presses the daughter under her skirt:

> I closed my eyes and felt my forehead press against the familiar –

something like wet of me, of looser spores, unexpectedly dry,
smelling of wet. 'Since you are so big,' she said,
'let me remind you –' and she told me with her body
that I was her child...

Bernard, like Maitreyabandhu, queers her childhood memory, taking the shamful hatred associated with female genitalia to imagine a visceral journey inside the mother's body to the source of her birth. The poem gives the poet a way to celebrate her mother's strength and self-love, and her own, born through her.

In 'Yogjakarta' Bernard pushes form to describe the gap between sexual desire and experience: the gap the narrator wants closed:

give me it, she did –
the sting   , I have wanted it,
I have spent, maybe five, maybe ten
years   waiting to be prised...

it's newness is
feeling full   , or going deaf
underwater , every sense
re-centred   , your gut is hollow....
why fear   , what you started?

The narrator's unsureness judders through the halting fragmented lineation and the discrete imagery. The poem's title recalls the Yogjakarta Principles of 2006 when full LGBT equality rights were confirmed in human rights legislation and, as the narrator considers that how she is defined would be punishable by death in Yemen, opening up the narrative to the wider global problematisation of queer love.

Slovenian poet Anja Golob also explores the gap between self-image and how one is seen. When having sex, the narrator experiences herself as alien as well as intimate, monstrous as much as tender and the articulations of these poignantly awkward ambivalences queer it for me. "She did not know I was a glow-worm but also had / long tentacles and a wax nest" she writes in 'Light Comes From Beneath' (Vesa V Zgibi, 2013). The poet goes on to describe the ache of wanting to be known while already experiencing inadequacy and the fear of its exposure.

It is written on my fingertips, but she did not notice.
It could be that I carry in my hands whatever it is she may love,
But it is more likely that I only have a flint stone and a handful of
    dry wood
And do not know how to use them to make them be fire.

In his forthcoming *Turtlemen*, Andra Simons also uses the powerful image of the mythical other – the turtleman – to denote his own strangeness. In '78/04' he travels between his childhood in Bermuda and adult London life, building his queer self out of his father's swimming and his mother's clothes to emerge, displaced out of his watery, tropical element but whole, knowing and resilient, for he has mastered the trick of how to "drown long enough":

> 1978
>
> whale boy / playing dead on the surface / flotsam floating out into the world made of television lights / drowning is a game based on time / my father rises out of the water / he has found the perfection in drowning / [...] like granny's superstitions he rises / [...] a positive dance through the negative space I swallow / "you gotta learn to not kick at the water" / become Turtlemen

> 2004
>
> I cut me mother's skirt and make underwear
> I wear them at popular London aquariums
> Where I wait for wild men to dive
> Crack my shell   a reflection of neon light on the surface tension
> I lost my home a long time ago
> Turtlemen know how to drown
> Long enough to crawl out onto the night beach [...]

In 'Swallowing Shorelines', the sexual act leaves the narrator yearning as he senses the lover's own distaste as he withdraws. Both "inside" and "outside", "within" and "without" are interchanged as the narrator speaks of sex as a kind of poison and the separation that he knows will ensue.

> "Hold this stone in your mouth." I bite down
> while he removes me from within like an
> allergy to the stars, like a toxin from the blood.

It is these tiny operations during which I fall.

"I can see the horizon just beyond your back,"
he says. Wanting more from the promising light,
I reach for the edge of his bed, respire and rise
toward the glow, a yearning outside.

Sophie Mayer's eight-part sequence *Incarnadine* delivers the wonderful, adventurous, direct and blisteringly funny voice of Medusa, a 6-9 year old intersex child whose mother, Cetys, discovers her enlarged clitoris when she's getting changed for a swim. Mayer invents an extraordinary sea-world, full of the punning and metaphoric richness of ambiguous and amphibious desire as a way to explore the chaotic feelings of a "little girl who had a little curl" and unruly sea-weedy hair. She was a "pigwolf, both goat and troll" she decides as her mother tries to pluck her chin.

No mention had been made of girls
with beards so maybe she was becoming a man. Or better yet, a
witch. Or goat, or god, or even a mussel.

The wobbly awe of puberty hitting early is captured in loose, mostly long lines, casual diction and immense rhythmic control.

Even underwater
she's a nuclear sun, bloody shark-bait
in a toosmall swimsuit. Hairs
and nipples everywhere! If this is sprouting, then
she's sprouting like a Venus Fly-Trap or
that plant which flowers once
a century and stinks of carrion.
She's nine years old and bleeding [...]

This is a bold, rollicking, clever and compassionate intersexual ballad with the wit and colour of an anime cartoon.

Caroline Bergvall calls herself a plurilingual, "binational, dispersed, ssipated [sic], French hyphen Norwegian writer" (*Cropper*, 2008). In her painful, passionate and urgent prose poem, 'Croup', Bergvall describes how writing in French deserted her after she was forbidden to see her teenage lover who bestowed the ability to speak: "Voila, she led me to the river, eau

eau pressed me down lifted my electric / brass [...] up-chemised / my shirt [...] couchd me safely / profoundly on this earth. Then placed a lump of saliva / on my tongue, and gave me language." Bergvall's love letter is found and the consequences mute her: "Nonono came the voices choral came the laws. / Loud vrbl hindrances, they tear through my mystries. Nono / no body be languaged sexd in this way, a crowd moves in." Her behaviour is policed, monitored. "How will I love –". Later through "conflicted blonging", "I could pass for someone, b perfectly dismulated..." until the sound of words, the aural pleasure grows and "riting resumes a root".

In relation to poets like Bergvall, Professor Susan Rudy argues for "poetries of enactment" where radical experimentation in language and form constantly challenges and renews perspective and categorisation. As Rudy suggests that queer in Bergvall's work refers not only to same-sex object choice or even to the fluidity of gender and sexuality, but also to what Bergvall calls "the open mesh of possibilities, lapses and excesses of meaning" that are rendered through this way of writing.

Is it something about being the other, being taught self-denial and self-hatred that makes queer poets alert to the consequences and cruelty of making someone the despised other? What I am increasingly drawn to in anthologies and collections by queer poets is an ethical poetry, a poetry that tries to inhabit the multiple other, the oppressed other from the painful experience of having been othered. This seems to open the way towards a poetry of compassion and empathy which returns queer to its original ant-discriminatory, fiery and important impulse.

Bergvall speaks of "the scrupulousness of poetry" by "a kind of fighter who doesn't fight by definition" (*Fig*, 2005). So let's not fight over definition. Keep it open. Keep it scrupulous.

Thanks to Nina Rapi for discussions around this essay.

Cherry Smyth is the author of three poetry collections, including *Test, Orange* (Pindrop Press, 2012). She is also an art critic.

𝓑

Walking Naked

NII AYIKWEI PARKES

Very often, when I am asked to speak on a panel about my literary, particularly poetic, influences and I begin talking about the music I listened to as a boy – how quickly night falls in Accra, the four-o-clock flower flexing to sleep almost precisely two hours before darkness prevails – people think I am drifting from the subject. On more than one occasion, a fellow panellist or a member of the audience has come up to me, pen in hand, asking for names of writers and titles of books, as though these details are pieces of a puzzle that will unravel my literary heritage. But, to me, poetry's link to cycles, to rhythm, to music cannot be severed. It matters that I grew up listening to Gyedu Blay Ambolley, Wulomei and a mish-mash of Western hits that played on the radio – that I could sing everything from Kenny Rogers to BDP to Immature. It matters that I could hear the muezzin in the distance at the same time as the sky was changing colour. It matters just as much as it matters that E.E. Cummings loved art and Wilfred Owen was a soldier. Literature is not separate from life. Poetry is influenced by quality of light, variations of sound, the weight of wind, as well as shapes on a page.

I had heard Langston Hughes's 'I've Known Rivers' years before I read it. When I fell in love with W.B. Yeats's 'He Wishes for the Cloths of Heaven', I had never seen it on the page before; I heard a gruff old man recite it at a gathering in Accra. I read Yeats years later, in 1993, having left Ghana, where one of the hit songs was about a man begging his ex-wife to return to him because his new wife doesn't know his habits, to study in the UK. That is when I added 'A Coat' to my list of favourite Yeats poems, whence the title of this essay. It is not an arbitrary choice. The first line of the poem reads, "I made my song a coat" – and, I believe, at its core, a poem is a song. Everything else, including judgements of quality, have to do with the coat – and everyone knows how easy it is to get comfortable with an outfit. The whole idea of BLACK-tie dinners and little BLACK dresses derives from that notion of comfort.

Cultural heritage is complex and no two people have identical heritage, but a set of people growing up under the same circumstances will have a greater degree of heritage overlap – enough to understand each other, perhaps share largely similar notions of quality. Effectively, if we are not continually expanding the gamut of our experience of the world, then any markers of quality we insist on are, actually, the marks of a limited coterie that share our experience. In fact, often, when we (we – the ethnic minority writers, we – the working class) are asked about our literary heritage – our quality markers, so to speak – what the askers are actually saying is "how are you like us?" For that reason, I normally refuse to answer. Because the question of quality rests on degrees of difference and it is easy for the line to blur, for people to dismiss the quality of your output when the truth is that you are different.

From my limited Ghanaian perspective, I am not convinced that enough poetry editors in the UK are mindful of the separation between quality and difference. I say 'limited Ghanaian' because my mythologies are uniquely mine: no other Ghanaian skipped school to watch Indian films and sang 'Yaadon Ki Baaraat' when he spotted his brother in a crowd, no other boy from Accra climbed into a mango tree to read Atukwei Okai's *Logorligi Logarithims*, no other boys sat on the immediate left of Egya Koo Nimo on a North Kaneshie Sunday playing a shaker while the legend sang. I could go on, but the list wouldn't illuminate my point any better. Some differences are harder for us to deal with than others, but that doesn't mean we shouldn't try. From my Ghanaian perspective, the stagnation in mainstream UK poetry publishing is due to a dearth in humility amongst editors, rather than a dearth of talent in the country. Two highly publicised open discussions have been held by literary organisation Spread The Word in the past seven years about the lack of publishing opportunities for ethnic minority poets, and not a single editor from Picador, Faber or Jonathan Cape (the best-funded poetry publishers) has attended. Editors are used to having the answers, recognising patterns and references (old mythologies), being the authority. But unearthing true creativity involves confronting the unfamiliar, giving and taking, being fallible. James Baldwin once wrote (in his essay 'Down at the Cross') that "if one cannot risk oneself, then one is simply incapable of giving". I would suggest that mainstream poetry editors in the UK haven't given us anything new in a long time; what they have served us, while good, has become so familiar that we have become numb to its flavour.

People in poetry (and the culture industry as a whole) often assume concerns about insularity are an issue of skin colour. They are not. A poet's skin colour has no bearing on how novel or unconventional their work is, their cultural construction does – the schools they went to, the music they are exposed to, the number of languages they speak, the poets they fall in love with. So arguments about presses being diverse based on the pigmentation of the poets they publish are not always valid; sometimes it's the equivalent of a restaurant redecorating without changing its menu.

Poetry is far more complex than skin colour. Yes, we live in a country where skin colour clearly demarcates a *possible* difference in culture, but colour should not lead the conversation – culture should. We should be talking about the cultural minority. We should be talking about the willingness of editors to expand their cultural palettes when assessing work – to risk themselves. If our standards of quality are tied to one – admittedly complex – stratum of European culture of criticism and appreciation, we are effectively being sponsored by the same makers of difference that justified the slave trade, the same anthropologists that labelled people savages simply because they could not understand them. What is easy is not necessarily right.

It is easy at this point in the debate to raise up some traditional African, Asian or Latin American model as an example of other ways to appreciate poetry, but I don't believe that moves poetry forward. It still falls into the pit of constructing a rigid reference, creating another point from which poetry stagnates. If, for example, I allude to Atukwei Okai's use of Ga occasional call-to-listen (summons) openings and breaks in his poems, I, in so doing, negate the bold creative flourish of whom he chooses to call – persons of historical significance from Nkrumah to Mies van der Rohe – which is actually the real innovation in his poetics. One does not dance for the monkey in the same way one dances for the lion. Thus, if Atukwei calls Mayakovsky to come and listen to his poem, it can and should affect the way we read it. Therefore, the poem is always alive, adapting to the cultural exposure of the reader, while maintaining readability outside the knowledge of the summoned listeners. Yet, when I mentioned this in a lecture once, the question I got back was "how do YOU use Ga summons in your work". That is the danger of positing other models; people think it means they understand everything – each poet's work must be considered independently.

Poetry is a mix of ease, difficulty, familiarity and strangeness; reading it with an assumption of knowledge, supreme confidence that we can classify even its strangeness, fails both the reader (the editor) and the writer. For the writers know not their own strangeness; their strangeness is normal to them – a poem that can be fully explained is an academic construct, not a poem. And, perhaps, learning is where our ailment comes from. Don Patterson, in a 2010 *Guardian* article on Shakespeare's sonnets, touched on the value of a primary – non-academic, if you will – reading. I don't believe many of us editors (yes, I'm shapeshifting) fully allow ourselves that luxury. In fact, now that I'm speaking from the editor's side, I am also inclined to believe that the place where UK poetry finds itself may be due to the editors loving poetry (in the incarnation they know) too much. Gilbert Murray, the Australian-British classical scholar, states in his essay 'Poesis and Mimesis' that "every generation has its blind spots". He goes on to note how poems revered in one generation are despised in another and to outline how certain poetic elements become more dominant than others, saying: "In England the eighteenth century poets learnt to write much smoother heroic couplets than Shakespeare or Ben Jonson... while they lost much of the art of writing blank verse." The blessing and tragedy of *our* generation is that education teaches us all that has come before, but also instructs us on what is 'good', fossilising ideas of 'quality' that were once much more fluid. The end result is that *mimesis* – imitation – supersedes *poêsis* – creation – as a marker of good poetry, the balance is skewed, and stagnation ensues.

A few years ago I was at an Association of Writers & Writing Program conference in the US. A poetry academic, reading one of my poems, commented that the first line was classic iambic pentameter and wondered why I hadn't continued the poem in that meter. I said that wasn't the music I was going for, explaining that while I taught 'traditional' meter, my own writing was influenced by my first language, Ga, West African highlife music and the experimentation culture of jazz. He asked that I speak some Ga and I did, whereupon he said, "Well, it's metered, I don't see what the problem is", going on to rant about how free verse had destroyed poetry. We had a long discussion during which I tried to remind him that nobody actually 'owned' poetry so it couldn't be protected, but he ended with what he considered to be a conclusive argument – that Derek Walcott writes in traditional meter.

Do you see what happened there? Blink and you've missed it – I don't think the academic even realised what he had done. I probably have more in common with a French-Swiss who grew up in German-speaking Switzerland, with a language in the home that differs substantially from the language of instruction. I will not even bring up the issue of Ga being – like Chinese – tonal as well as metrical. For all the melanin abundance that Walcott and I share, we don't have the same linguistic heritage – even if one extrapolates his origins back to Ghana, one still has more than 60 languages to choose from. But extrapolation is not lived reality and the academic's comment is still simply an ill-conceived conclusion based on outer appearances – the coat, not the song. Besides, to attempt to distill Walcott's brilliance down to the use of traditional meter is just plain – what's a kind word? – misguided. Needless to say, really, I ended the conversation there.

Harold Bloom speaks of great poetry having "one broad and essential difficulty", which it accomplishes through strangeness. My observation is that, on the whole, mainstream editors in the UK fear certain kinds of strangeness – of class, of gender, of literary culture. They have become the plaintive husband in the song I left in Ghana in 1993, who, no sooner has his new wife moved in, starts begging the old one – the one who knows his habits – to come back, calling for the old coat, so to speak. The result is that, bar the odd jump when a new coat is held up briefly in the mirror to admire, mainstream poetry output has flat-lined. That is no comment on the overall health of poetry publishing in the UK. Small presses are doing a fabulous job; this year's Forward Prize for Best First Collection is dominated by them – Peepal Tree Press's *The Twelve-Foot Neon Woman* by Loretta Collins Klobah and Seren's *Clueless Dogs* by Rhian Edwards are fresh, exciting reads. The final question, I suppose, is where is my authority in all this – this Ghanaian from a fishing family born in a British fishing town? I don't kid myself; I have no authority. I am like one of those Western observers sent to places like Zimbabwe to comment on the fairness of elections; I can say what I think but whether or not it changes anything is anyone's guess. As an observer, I believe I am qualified: although I am no literature graduate, I have read poetry all my life – I have read the writers most British pupils read in school in addition to African poets such as Christopher Okigbo, David Rubadiri, Okot p'Bitek, Aquah Laluah, Mazisi Kunene – each with their own unique ways of expressing the sum of their heritage – and a whole swathe of non-European poets. As an editor, I see new contemporary work every day. But these qualifications are mere embroideries on my coat. As an observer I come to the poetry with naked ear or naked eye and wait to be moved, perhaps, to be clothed anew.

Nii Ayikwei Parkes is Senior Editor at flipped eye publishing, author of *The Makings of You* (Peepal Tree Press) and a 2007 recipient of Ghana's national ACRAG award for poetry and literary advocacy.

REVIEWS

ℬ

I reject the temptation to see this as something of a subtle re-colonisation, but choose instead to remind myself of how porous the walls of culture, identity and geography are in the contemporary space.

– *Kwame Dawes*

Two Substantial Anthologies

KWAME DAWES

Out of Bounds, eds. Jackie Kay, James Proctor & Gemma Robinson,
Bloodaxe, £12, ISBN 9781852249298
The Harper Collins Book of English Poetry, ed. Sudeep Sen,
Harper Collins India, Rs.599, ISBN 9789350290415

Despite the number of anthologies I have edited with glee, I confess I have a strange anxiety about anthologies. They overwhelm me. The larger they are, the more overwhelmed I feel. The feeling is similar to the sensation of entering a major metropolitan art gallery full of master works. I don't know where to start. I panic, and then I become distressed about my inability to process what I am seeing. Of course I keep going to these galleries and I keep leaving with a sense that I have benefited from the experience. It helps when the gallery is a good one – well-designed and full of striking work. The good news is that these two anthologies manage to justify their existence on that basis as well.

Out of Bounds, edited by Jackie Kay, James Proctor and Gemma Robinson, makes as compelling a case as I have seen that there is a vibrant and accomplished body of poetry by Black and Asian poets in the UK. It is a substantial book and it features one hundred and thirty poets, several of whom are represented by two or three poems. The book does feel cramped, the font noticeably small, and the compactness makes reading harder than one would want, but it is the price one pays, I suppose. Of course, as the editors point out, the anthology does not attempt to be a canon-building project. Instead, it remains committed to its conceptual framework, which is represented by the title of the collection: *Out of Bounds*. The editors do not devote a great deal of space to the possible readings of the term, allowing me to indulge a little here.

"Out of bounds" is a term normally associated with sports – when a ball goes outside of the play area demanding a stoppage of the game and a restart from the sidelines, one says that the ball is "out of bounds". The idea, then, is that these writers who might have existed outside the mainstream of British life, have managed to turn that position into a viable and exciting place – a kind of counter presence that redefines the lines of separation that exist. Thus, the idea of transgression, border crossing, and alternate thinking and creativity are all evoked by the title.

However, the editors seem keen on having us pay more attention to the idea of space and place than is implied by the title. The anthology is structured deliberately around the idea of the British geographic space, such that the sections of the work replicate the map of the UK. First, the three British nations, Scotland, Wales and England are represented. Scotland and Wales get their own sections, while England is represented by its regions: North, Midlands and South.

This organising system allows them to make a most critical point – that all of Britain has been fully 'colonised' by these Black and Asian poets through their physical and imaginative occupation of the space. Typically, the idea of Black and Asian presence has largely been assumed to be isolated to the south of England – namely London.

Rather than propose that the poets 'belong' to any of these locales – either by their residency or by their claims of some national or regional loyalty, thus allowing the editors to elect anything by those poets from each region for inclusion – the editors instead have collected poems that actually engage with the idea of place – poems that speak about these regions and help us envision these spaces through the prism of race and identity.

This allows them to produce a book that, while wonderfully reflective of some of the exciting poets writing today in the UK, also includes selections that date as far back as Una Marson, the Jamaican poet whose heyday was during the nineteen forties and fifties in the UK. The anthology also features Louise Bennett, Kamau Brathwaite, George Lamming (who began his career as a poet), Wole Soyinka and John Figueroa. The benefit of their inclusion is that it establishes that there is a fairly long and evolving tradition of Black and Asian poets writing in and about Britain. The selections help us to observe the movement from the experiences of the immigrants of the forties and fifties and those of the British-born Black and Asian poets who are busy redefining what Britain is.

Another curious decision made by the authors is not to get preoccupied with the matter of nationality and residency. This allows them to include the work of poets such as Derek Walcott and Lorna Goodison, neither of whom has actually lived in the UK for an extended period of time. Yet their poems fall under what the editors deftly describe as the "global communities caught in Britain's imperial past and present".

One does get the sense, however, that the editors simply sought to find rich, dynamic and compellingly written poems that offer an insight into the idea of Britain, like the amusing 'Do' Care' by Bashabi Fraser who writes of a daughter negotiating the complex issue of national loyalties in a girl of multiple heritages and 'homes', through an examination of sports fandom. When the stakes are highest, she will take no sides, because she "do' care" who wins when the teams she loves are competing. I choose to mention this poem of almost two hundred collected here because it somehow captures exactly my feeling about the collection – and here the phrase "do' care" does not mean that I don't care about the idea of the collection, the execution of the collection or the achievement of the collection, but that I admire the work so much that I don't care to spend time quibbling about who might have been left out (Fifi Anobil of Wales, Janet Kofi Tsekpo and many others) and/or who might have been included, since at the end of the day I find this a convincing read.

Without meaning to be, *Out of Bounds* has become the most comprehensive gathering of Black and Asian British poets in any single volume, and in this the editors have done a great service. I have found it annoyingly impossible to single out poems and poets, but I have to say that I have found myself remarking at the high quality of the work selected and the effective way in which the editors engage place and identity, complicating the very idea of Britishness.

Sudeep Sen, in his introduction to *The Harper Collins Book of English Poetry*, seems to suggest that the phenomenon of Indian Poetry in English is a relative young one – arguably as old as the modern nation of India. He says that his decision to collect the work of poets born after nineteen fifty, represents his attempt to establish a marker of the emergence of Indian poetry in English, one that nicely marks out a piece of territory around which to draw some conclusions about the poetry produced. By titling the collection *The Harper Collins Book of English Poetry*, something quite bold is taking place. The publishers, one can only assume, are arguing that this anthology constitutes a major contribution to poetry in English and one that should be appreciated for its global authority. I am reminded of Chinua Achebe's provocative reminder that "English is a Nigerian language". One gets a taste of Sen's discriminating eye in the selections of some of the stand-out poets collected. And while these are the poets whose reputations we know well, there is no guarantee that the selections will do them justice. In this anthology Meena Alexander, David Dabydeen, Vikram Seth, Sujata Bhatt, Raman Mundair, Priya Sarukkai Chabira, Michelle Cahill, Menka Shivdasani, and, of course, Sen himself, are all represented by some stunning poems. Of special note are Chabria's long sequence 'Everyday Things in my Life' and Mundair's very necessary 'Chattri Yatra'.

I remain fascinated by how unselfconsciously so many of the poets 'own' and co-opt the idioms and the mythologies of western literary practice, and how authoritative is their command of this source – such that western classical music, politics, literature, mythology and popular culture become elemental to their poetics. I reject the temptation to see this as something of a subtle re-colonisation, but choose instead to remind myself of how porous the walls of culture, identity and geography are in the contemporary space. The poets collected here live all over the world, many of them were born in cultures other than India, and most, like much of the world, find themselves citizens of a complex and information-rich world of the internet, international travel and migration. The poetry reflects this. In this sense, one would be hard-pressed (as I suspect Sen himself is, explaining why he punts the task of trying to construct an aesthetic or some kind of literary mapping of modern Indian poetry to "academics and scholars" and, one supposes, reviewers) to somehow unearth some essential 'Indian poetic' from this anthology. And yet, if one is prepared to accept the idea of openness, a broad imaginative palette gladly embracing all orthodoxies and in so doing dismantling them, as the defining character of what we see collected here, then we may, in fact have arrived at a functional aesthetic. It makes sense, for instance, that the British-born Daljit Nagra seems far more fascinated by the meaning of being Indian than any of the poets who live and write in India.

I can only point to some highlights in a volume of more than five hundred pages and representing eighty-five poets. There is an intellectual energy and daring in Jeet Thayil's work – the irresistible danger of confession and wisdom ("It's an affliction to grow up motherless, with your lady mother / living beside you" ('Letter from a Mughal Emperor 2006'). His honesty is sometimes alarming: "When you said, 'I mean it, we live like stones,'/ you broke something in me only heroin / could fix" ('Heroin Sestina'). I am inclined to go searching for more work by this poet, as I am to find the first full-length collection of Judith Lal, whose poems collected here have an assurance of idea, but more importantly, a kind of hunger for the world – a capacity to be surprised, puzzled and engaged by the world. It is a contagious thing. See her poem 'Chit' to see what I mean. Another tantalisingly interesting voice is Monica Moody, a fairly young poet whose experiments with syntax and versification sharpen her interest in politics and the personal intersecting in fruitfully troubling ways. Here she is on Delhi: "I stuff // the feeling into my mouth / become a crow // device to scratch throats / trash bins" ('I, Or'). I will resort now to listing a few names of poets whose work I am committed to seeking out having been introduced to them here. The list would include Sridala Swami, Deepankar Khiwani ('Life on the Island'), Chitra Banerjee Divakaruni ('After Death: A Landscape'), Bibhu Padhi ('Someone Has Been Missing'), Bhanu Kapil ('Schizophrene'), Robin S. Ngangom (if only for the line, "Only poetry of ruins is real"), Subhashini Kaligotla ('Reading Plato'), Vikas K. Menon (whose 'Pyre' is simply arresting) and Anindita Sengupta whose metaphors are startling:

A backyard of bramble and weed was where

we found noise. It wandered knock-kneed
and had a tongue full of pins. ('Brink')

Knowing Sen's work, I see his fingerprints all over this extremely beautiful book with its striking cover image. The poems are given space to breathe, and the small details – the tiny symbols, the deft font choices, and the generous use of title pages to showcase the poets – give this book a quality of care and taste that is enviable.

For all the amazing work in these two anthologies, what impresses most is the monumental accomplishment of the editors. Sen has been at this for a while and he should be recognised for his tireless efforts as an editor of numerous poets under his quite successful small imprint Aark Arts, and as the dogged editor of many anthologies of Indian poetry that constantly make the case for a lively and engaging poetic movement coming out of India and its diaspora. This volume is a culmination of that work – a work of care, thoroughness and generosity. Kay, Proctor and Robinson did not take the easy route of just tossing a bunch of poems together for their anthology – instead, they found a thematic focus that would be broad enough to allow for comprehension and representation, and narrow enough to make our reading discoveries fresh as we plow through all those pages. In the end they have not cured me of my fear of anthologies, but they have at least confirmed what I have always suspected: that anthologies remain extremely necessary in this business.

Kwame Dawes is a poet and writer of fiction, non-fiction, criticism and drama. He is the Glenna Luschei Editor of *Prairie Schooner* and a Chancellor's Professor of English at the University of Nebraska. His *Duppy Conqueror: New and Selected Poems* will be published by Copper Canyon in 2013.

B

Is Poetry The 'Real Mother Tongue'?

SARADHA SOOBRAYEN

The Parley Tree, An Anthology of poets from French-speaking Africa and the Arab World, ed. Patrick Williamson, with Yann Lovelock, Arc, £12.99, ISBN 9781906570613;
Bones Will Crow, An Anthology of Burmese Poetry, ed. and trans. by ko ko thett and James Byrne, Arc, £12.99, ISBN 9781906570897

The parley tree (*arbre á palabres*), also known as the baobab tree, can live over a thousand years and has survived atrocities spanning lifetimes, as on Gorée island, off Dakar in Senegal, a major landmark in the history of slavery: the final African stop for slaves bound for the Americas. One of the recent additions to Arc Publications's bilingual translation anthology series takes its name from this emblematic tree.

Editor and translator Patrick Williamson presents a linguistic map of diverse poetries in French, unconfined by geographical and political borders. This anthology showcases established poets from Algeria, Cameroon, Chad, Congo Brazzaville, Democratic Republic of Congo, Djibouti, Ivory Coast, Lebanon, Mauritius, Morocco, Senegal and Tunisia. These contemporary poets are rooted in the French language but are haunted by 'open wounds' from the colonial aftermath, and united and divided through their complex relationship with the language of the oppressor, and the language of liberty and exile.

Through this they have developed a *lingua franca* poetry, coexisting uneasily at times alongside the many mother tongues and national languages, including Arabic, Fula, Bambara, Berber, Wolof and Mauritian Creole as in the work of Khal Torabully, whose long discursive poem, 'Hold full of stars, Coolitude', ends in a telling question:

> Coolitude: because I am Creole through my rigging, Indian
> by my mast, European by the yard, Mauritian through quest and
> French through exile. I will only be elsewhere in my self
> because my native land exists only as I imagine...

> Is that why poetry is my real mother tongue?

This is an example of the complex identity emerging through the language, a shared history of displacement that is both common and hidden. Hence the term "coolitude", coined by Torabully, to signify the ownership of a mosaic identity, stemming back to the derogatory term used for indentured labourers: coolie.

In his preface the poet Tahar Bekri comments that:

> Such a project is aimed primarily at doing away with the divisions and distinctions between countries of the same continent [...] the poets themselves have long wished to be associated with common threads and to escape artificial and suspect pigeon-holing, which has long been imposed by fairly reductive historical literary division.

Much of the commonality in imagery found within the poetry is rooted within the language of landscape. Poetry reclaiming and restoring the elemental features of colonised lands, ravaged by wars. The recurring image through many of the poets' work is of the baobab or parley tree, which signifies a traditional meeting place for communities to converse and tell stories, creating dialogue that ranges from complaint to reconciliation. The opening of Senegal-born Amadou Lamine Sall's Whitman-like long poem 'My Country is not a dead country' sees this place in shadow:

> My country is not a nocturnal baobab
> blackened grass a cold flower
> anemic fruit a land on its knees
> My country is not a road cut off
> a pot-holed surfaced a muddy sky
> my country is not the pressing need of vultures

Born in Abidjan, Ivory Coast, Tanella Boni is one of the three featured women poets, alongside Amina Said (Tunisia) and Venus Khoury-Ghata (Lebanon). They are well suited to tackling the larger themes of war and the legacy of slavery as witnessed by the baobab trees in Tanella Boni's delicate and powerful four-poem sequence 'Goreé Baobab Island':

> perhaps happiness is so far away
> invisible among the tamarind leaves
> when my hand brushes the fruit
> to share them with spirits laughing at man's

cruelty to man
perhaps the hope in my eyes drags
the future in clouds of dust where I seek
sparks and the dignity of condemned souls

This poem is an example of the way in which *The Parley Tree* offers a blend of lyricism, anger, humility and intellect, through a rich tapestry of inherited influences and styles that infuses the text of the poems. These translations offer English speakers the flavour of distinct voices moving through the French language, which lends itself to being shaped in a variety of forms, ranging between the longer lines, sequences and shorter lyrics that explore philosophical moments of being.

The release of *Bones Will Crow* by Arc Publications coincides with the recent human rights developments in Burma. The mouths of poets have been and continue to be silenced. Poets and non-poets are imprisoned, tortured and made to disappear silently at the hands of oppressive regimes which are all too happy to utilise the power of poetic thought and rhetorical language to mobilise armies and justify crimes against humanity in Burma.

This is a highly-anticipated anthology of fifteen diverse Burmese poets spanning several generations, whose contribution to the continual fight against the suppression of democracy and free speech is even more necessary now. These poets are essential reading for the wider world for their historical perspective and experimental approaches to poetry and poetics.

The poet Zeyar Lynn was a featured poet as part of the Southbank Centre's recent Poetry Parnassus festival and is widely regarded as the most influential poet in Burma. His poetic practice has been informed by and reacted to the changing political struggles within Burma and around the world:

No tomb, no bone
Not even ash
I have not written my history
They have written it for me, those academics
[...]
They have written even my own death
Amid deaths and deader deaths   (From 'My History is Not Mine')

Like many of his contemporaries, Zeyar Lynn sought to create innovative poetries that traveled beyond the different movements that challenged the status quo and British colonialism. These movements included

Khitpyaing, meaning contemporary or "parallel with the times" and *Khitsan*, "testing the times". He is renowned for developing a Burmese poetics that is located in the head rather than the heart, in sync with the development of L=A=N=G=U=A=G=E poetic forms and post-modern experimentalism.

The 'turn to language' by non-conformist writers provokes an uneasy dialogue with the once avant garde, now mainstream, modernist Khitpor writers whose poets are forced to face their own limitations and endorse the new generations of poets who continue to play a crucial part in the development of Burmese political and cultural life.

Ruth Padel's illuminating foreword highlights the role of Rangoon University and the Burmese student population that led the nationalist protest against the British in the nineteen twenties and more recently the fatal mass rally against the oppressive military regime in the nineteen eighties. Aung Cheimt's futuristic-looking poem 'You will read' is a reminder of the sacrifices made, and the need for the profound and the ordinary to once again coalesce:

> In the future
> things will be enigmatic and profound
> exclamations will be used
> onomatopoeia will be used
> [...]
> you will read
>
> We read, take notes, study
> we write.
> We write, study, take notes,
> we read
> We read, take notes, study
> we write.

The spirit of Buddhism resides at the core of the writing of later generations of poets such as ko ko thett, who speaks of the emptiness of tyranny in deceptively playful lines:

> I am a chilli, you are a lime
> other people are bitter gourds
> the empire is overstretched
> the emperor is overdressed

denizens wear nothing but the loin cloth
of law, it's no progression, it's a draw

This uncensored voice appears in another poem by ko ko thett, 'The burden of being Bama', which refers to the difficulty of being a member of the majority ethnic group in Burma:

what would you choose
want, rage or ignorance
defeatism or *maldevelopment*

Poems like these demand a response from the reader. There is no hiding or denying our call to respond to these poems in translation, which offer the opportunity to further understand ourselves in relation to another.

The poems of *Bones Will Crow* exist in their own right and should be treated with the same deference that we afford poets who are more familiar and less complex. The contradictory and imposing forces that shape Burmese poetry continue to create an evolving poetics that courageously redefines and reasserts itself, both internally and externally, to the wider literate world.

Saradha Soobrayen is a freelance poetry editor and coach, and is a trustee of *Modern Poetry in Translation*.

The Poetry Society seeks to appoint

EDITOR
POETRY REVIEW

beginning spring 2013

For full details, visit the *Poetry Review*
section of the Poetry Society website:
www.poetrysociety.org.uk/content/publications/review

Or email: info@poetrysociety.org.uk

THE
POETRY
SOCIETY

Around the World in 204 Countries

MICHAEL HOROVITZ

The World Record: International Voices from Southbank Centre's
Poetry Parnassus, ed. Neil Astley & Anna Selby, Bloodaxe,
£10, ISBN 9781852249380

T*he World Record* is the accompanying and surviving 'Hymn & Her Book' of the Poetry Parnassus festival, featuring poets from two hundred and four countries, which jam-packed the Southbank Centre (SBC) throughout the last week of June 2012. This international gathering was conceived by SBC director Jude Kelly with its poet-in-residence Simon Armitage, and delivered by the Centre's Literature & Spoken Word team, coordinated by Anna Selby. Selby's Co-Editor of the printed *World Record* is one of Britain's most prolific anthologists, Bloodaxe boss Neil Astley.

Armitage's Introduction, which has slightly pruned and updated his 'Poetry Parnassus' manifesto in *Poetry Review* 102: 2, stating that one poet from each nation taking part in the London Olympic Games was "identified … some decidedly literary, others from storytelling, oral or performing traditions, some world famous, others barely known outside their own borders (and some hardly known within them either). Parnassus developed into a week of readings, translations, conferences, workshops, discussions, arguments and all things poetic". Selby's preface summarises the administrative gestation of the festival, and reveals that six thousand nominations of potential participants were received after four months of their having been solicited.

There follow two hundred and sixty pages of texts – one by each poet – presented in alphabetical order of their respective countries of origin, and seventy pages of biographical notes along with acknowledgements for each contribution. Among the two hundred and four, Australia is represented by John Kinsella, both Brunei Darussalam and the Central African Republic by Anonymous, Great Britain by Jo Shapcott, Ireland by Seamus Heaney, Ukraine by Serhiy Zhadan and the Russian Federation by Ukraine-bred Ilya Kaminsky. The latter has been living in the US since being granted asylum there in 1993, and now writes in English. Around fifteen of the poets included have been based in the UK for some time, and a similar number in

North America. No indication is given as to how these Parnassians were selected, beyond Armitage's avowal that they were ones "whose work excited us and whose presence we hoped would bring energy and integrity to this curated project".

The book is appropriately dedicated "to all translators". But the quality of many of the texts, all published in English only, feels pretty uneven to me. Without knowledge of the original language versions of those which have been translated, it's difficult to intimate what may have been lost or gained in each case. Nevertheless, Valzhyna Mort's translated 'Belarusian 1' is one of a number of poems which engage with contemporary atrocities, and are as compelling for their diction, cadences and imagistic drive as for the devastating experiences they convey: "even our mothers have no idea how we were born / how we parted their legs and crawled out into the world / the way you crawl from the ruins after a bombing / we couldn't tell which of us was a girl or a boy / we gorged on dirt thinking it was bread // [...] we discovered we ourselves were the language / and when our tongues were removed we started talking with our eyes / and when our eyes were poked out we talked with our hands / and when our hands were cut off we conversed with our toes / and when we were shot in the legs we nodded our heads for yes / and shook our heads for no and when they ate our heads alive / we crawled back into the bellies of our sleeping mothers / as if into bomb shelters / to be born again".

Israeli Anat Zecharya's translated dramatic monologue, 'A Woman of Valour', strikes a more documentary stance. Epigraphed by a newsflash that more than thirty-five soldiers and civilian employees at an airbase had been abusing a fourteen-year-old girl for a year, it recounts how "The first / places your head on his naked lap / and one might think / you weren't being forced but rather / thanked and your head stroked. / The second slides slowly down your back / and feelings are new / and you can still concentrate. // The third inserts three fingers, says / 'Don't move.' You don't, / the map of greater Israel / in your eyes. / The fourth moves aside a pile of reports / on air accidents in the south / and takes you from behind [...] The unstoppable fifth and sixth / course into you. / The arrogant salt of the earth, avoiding eyes, / those waiting their turn. Soon your body may look beautiful / even to you."

The focused graphic rapportage of 'I Sell My Daughter for 100 Won' by North Korean Jang Jin Seong; 'History Project' by Marshall Islands/Hawaiian Kathy Jetnil-Kijner; 'London Bombings' by Yuyutsu Sharma from Nepal; and 'We Teach Life, Sir' by London-based Palestinian refugee Rafeef Ziadah, are similarly mind-stilling. But quite a lot of *The World Record*'s other (a)political rages and rants fall a lot flatter than these in cold print (effective though some of them might seem in the heat of agit-prop gatherings or would-be revolutionary demonstrations, or the partisan euphoria of Slams). The tensions between playing to more or less easily won over galleries of potential fellow rebels or fans, and capturing the "true voice of feeling", seem more often blurred than not here – which may be a recurrent difficulty around the overcrowded joustings of much performance poetry worldwide.

The World Record presents a goodly cache of diversely accomplished prose poems, as well as a precious few pieces – such as the South African Katharine Kilalea's 'You were a bird', and Spain's Eli Tolaretxipi's 'Still Life with Loops' – whose pure lyric impulses do not sooner or later dissolve into anger, desolation, or sheer fear and loathing. Or, still more rarely, as in 'Garden' by Hamid Ismailov (who was forced to flee Uzbekistan, where his works are banned, for London in 1992), into stoical or oblique acceptance of the limitations and inhumanities of humankind. Although traditional western notions of high poetic standards may be confounded by a largeish fraction of the translated texts, there can be little denying that there are few which do not articulate down-to-earth realism, a far cry from the frequently chauvinistic-nationalistic triumphalism of the supposed glories of the so-called sporting Olympiads.

The few days of the Poetry Parnassus week I was able to spend at the SBC for the most part charmed me into staying a lot longer than I had planned to. Apart from the staggering variety of everywhere voluble wordsounds, the spontaneous comradeship between so many hitherto unbefriended as well as long befriended, albeit more usually far-flung writer-performers, was enormously refreshing – akin to a specifically poetic kind of mini-Glastonbury or Woodstock. And this communitarian spirit breathes through most pages of this anthology, even where various caveats may seem to qualify it.

Simon Armitage's Introduction to *The World Record* acknowledges that Poetry Parnassus was not entirely unprecedented, but built on "the SBC's Poetry International Festival, inaugurated in the '60s by Ted Hughes amongst others, and with a nod in the direction of the landmark and legendary 1965 Albert Hall event which went down in history as 'the Poetry Olympics'." This self-styled 'First International Poetry Incarnation' (filmed by Peter Whitehead as *Wholly Communion*), which I had a hand in organising, certainly helped put national and supra-national performances on the up-till-then pretty unpopulated map for the oral verse muses in Britain. The Poetry Olympics festivals were only formally launched as such fifteen years later, but the 1965 megagig was a prime precursor.

In my editorial to *New Departures 12*, the issue which doubled as a programme for the initial September 1980 Poetry Olympics in Westminster

Abbey, I mooted some "tentative objectives" of what our Poets' Cooperative hoped might follow: "To found a Poetry Olympics Council, or at least reach some agreement towards a future for these internationalist impulses. To get poets themselves more involved in organising our labour – the means and range of its distribution and reception across the globe. To contemplate four-year cycles of relatively small events, hosted by leading poets in their native lands, culminating in a more substantial quadrennial gathering, admission to which qua performer might have to be restricted by consensus considerations of the proven poetic track records of would-be Poetry Olympians."

Though some of these ambitions have not been realised, Poetry Olympics has, throughout each subsequent decade, presented many hundreds of events all over Britain, and occasionally abroad – large, middling and small. Now that Poetry Parnassus has picked up the baton, let us hope that further concerted global poetic interactions and extensions take place, toward ever-improving world records.

Let these reignited sacred flames keep burning bright. As Hughes wrote sixty-five years ago: "It is in poetry that we can refresh our hope that world unity is occupying people's imaginations everywhere, since poetry is the voice of spirit and imagination and all that is potential, as well as of the healing benevolence that used to be the privilege of the gods [...] It is not enough to say this once. It has to be said afresh year after year, in as many places and different languages as possible. And the effort of poets themselves to live up to their calling has to be renewed, year after year."

Michael Horovitz is currently fundraising to publish *The POE! (Poetry Olympics Enlightenment)* and *Great-Grandchildren of Albion* anthologies; to collate the far-flung New Departures archive; and to put together ever more diverse Poetry Olympics festivals. www.poetryolympics.com

ℬ

UNIVERSITY OF OXFORD — Continuing Education

MSt in Creative Writing

A two-year, part-time degree with 7 Residences and 1 Placement

Apply by 18 January 2013

mstcreativewriting@conted.ox.ac.uk
or see www.conted.ox.ac.uk/mstcw

Emotional Undercurrents

KAREN McCARTHY WOOLF

Tishani Doshi, *Everything Begins Elsewhere*, Bloodaxe,
£8.95, ISBN 9781852249366;
James Lasdun, *Water Sessions*, Cape, £10, ISBN 9780224097093;
Seni Seneviratne, *The Heart of It*, Peepal Tree, £8.99, ISBN 9781845231903

Welsh-Gujarati poet Tishani Doshi's *Everything Begins Elsewhere* takes its name from a phrase in John Burnside's memoir *A Lie About My Father*. Burnside is one of a number of presiding spirits who hover over this book of two halves, which commences with 'Everything Begins' and concludes with 'Elsewhere', a section prefaced by a quote from Italo Calvino's *Invisible Cities*. Doshi also responds to Pablo Neruda's *Walking Around* and Elizabeth Bishop's *The Art of Losing* in poems of the same names.

Loss – of a lover, parent, sense of self – is a recurrent theme. While Doshi's *Art of Losing* ponders the subject in a tone reminiscent of the original, it is the sestina 'Memory of Wales' that, through its repetitive form, seems to shake out a more raw, energised voice:

> Bronze cliffs in the distance sing. My mother
> has met a man. She's going away. I'm eight,
> but I've always known she'll leave all this.
> Forsaking, after all, is a kind of memory.

Doshi's mellifluous lyricism is heady and seductive, and hers is a landscape characterised as much by sound as it is image: whether it's a dog barking, crows squawking on her parents' window sill or a "creaking bougainvillea", as in the travelogue 'In Cartegena', where the poet sets out "looking for love / along cobbled streets" only to find Madras, the city of her birth. Place, or rather a liminal 'placelessness', is deeply embedded here – as is an undercurrent of restlessness that courses through the book like a river.

James Lasdun also explores profound emotional territory through the medium of water. His fourth collection, *Water Sessions*, dedicated to the memory of his father, is intense, intelligent and authentically complex, by which I mean there is a translucent layering of ideas, where the poetry of the intimate moment is exploded into a deeper psychological and political enquiry.

Many of the poems are vivified by the push and pull of supposedly opposing forces: what might be a purely cinematic or pastoral approach is unsettled by shifting realities, as in 'Storm', where gravestones are mistaken for tree-stumps. Likewise mythical and Biblical characters are displaced into contemporary domestic tableaux: in 'Blues for Samson' the poet visits his hairdresser "Dee", who "knows her middle-aged man; / playing me like some trailer Delilah, / and I feel it rise; // the old blunt / want-instrument."

In the titular three-part sequence, 'Water Sessions', the author tells his therapist about a fight with his partner where she throws water at him. Lasdun uses the patient–therapist dialogue as a multi-functional structural device: it supports yet playfully undermines the confessional endeavour as the poet struggles to contextualise himself as an 'Anglo-American-Jew' and, through the use of the therapist's interjections, simultaneously disrupts and propels the narrative.

> I might indeed wish to reconcile, even equate
> certain opposites; villain and victim
>
> tourist and terrorist; spitter even, and spat-at...
> – *Which brings us back, does it not,*
> *to your fight. I think you should really* –
>
> – Like I said, who ever knows what a fight was about?
> You go in thinking it's oil or land, and then later
> discover it was all along only ever
>
> about water...

Whether he is appealing to the ghost of his father, or in conversation with his six-year-old son, this is a book bursting with fruitful contradiction that takes on our essential philosophical predicaments with generosity and grace.

While Lasdun occupies the patient role in the drama, Seni Seneviratne, a qualified NHS psychotherapist, inhabits both personas in her second collection, *The Heart of It*. Having spent many years working with victims of abuse and trauma, she has the rare ability to give voice to the dispossessed while managing to avoid patronising the subject in the process.

This empathic approach is exemplified in 'Wounds of War', a poem that reveals the shocking statistic that the average number of "completed suicides per month" amongst US veterans from Iraq and Afghanistan is six hundred and ninety.

There is an I in this poem who is
as silent as the startled tulips, who can't
reach the imagined chime of where was it

he was heading before, before all this dust...

The 'I' becomes the voice of many, but never at the poem's expense: Seneviratne combines a delicate evocation of sensory detail with a steady gaze, no matter how harrowing the content. In 'Operation Cast Lead', a poem shortlisted for the Arvon International Poetry Prize, an unnamed Palestinian mother, who "thinks the guns are like / heavy limbs in the hands / of these wild-eyed boys" is shot dead in Gaza at the moment of turning "left instead of right, the sniper's eye holding her heart /at the centre of his lens".

The book is divided into two parts, with the more political work occurring in the second half. The initial section is, like Doshi's *Everything Begins Elsewhere*, part travelogue, part personal lyric. Set in Rome, Paris, New York and Cape Town as well as her native Leeds, these are poems of longing and regret that move from the pain of separation to a resurrection of self in the final poem of the section 'Easter Sunday' in which "the Adonis Blue butterfly, making / a cautious comeback, is poised above the vetch."

Karen McCarthy Woolf's collection *An Aviary of Small Birds* is forthcoming from Carcanet OxfordPoets.

ℬ

Poetry & Writing Courses
at
Château Ventenac

Poetry & creative writing workshops
as well as our popular writing retreats

Inspiring location beside the Canal du Midi
Spectacular views over vineyards to the Pyrenees
Lovely gardens and pool, great food
We look after you whilst you relax and write.

www.chateaulifecourses.com
Call Julia on +44 (0) 7773 206344
email: julia@chateaulifecourses.com

Château Life
Inspirational Creative Escapes

Tutors for 2013 include:

Sean O'Brien   Jo Bell

Tiffany Murray   Pascale Petit

The Most Beautiful Thing

ALISON BRACKENBURY

Helen Dunmore, *The Malarkey*, Bloodaxe, £8.95, ISBN 9781852249403;
Nina Bogin, *The Lost Hare*, Anvil, £8.95, ISBN 9780856464454;
Chrissie Gittins, *I'll Dress One Night as You*, Salt, £8.99,
ISBN 9780954328849;
Cherry Smyth, *Test, Orange*, Pindrop, £9.99, ISBN 9780956782274

The *Malarkey*'s epigraph is Sappho's: "The most beautiful thing on this dark earth". Helen Dunmore's compelling collection is haunted by darkness, which, one poem claims, "goes on for ever". Her intense prose account of Keats's death ends by night, "one candle burning".

The Malarkey also compels by mystery. Dunmore's prizewinning title poem circles its subject: children, left in a car, possibly dead. Energy of pace and dramatic address only strengthen a horrifying strangeness: "You looked away just once [...] and forty years were gone".

Dunmore's poems are patterned strongly, with commanding repetition: "Come out now and stand beside me". Muted half-rhymes mirror uncertainty: "me / asleep". Yet she can also rhyme memorably, as in 'Boatman', which itself echoes a folksong:

> and I say, hold tight to my hand
> for the water is wide where we stand.

The Malarkey is veined by a sense of evil. Even a slippery hill is "wicked". But Dunmore's work is complex, as stylistic shifts suggest. Dark days are "dear to me / as a bully to his mother". The voice of 'The Gift' could be her poems':

> I'm here, it told me
> to make you know things
> but not their names.

In her penultimate poem, singing is heard by night:

> in a blackbird's cold
> liquid delight, and so I turned
> on the landing, and you were gone.

Love, unnamed, is held against dark. Her final poem promises: "I won't [...] write another word". Dunmore, who conveys menace and mystery so powerfully, knows the value of silence.

Nina Bogin, born in the US, long resident in France, writes beautiful, spare, exemplary poems from which everything unnecessary is quietly stripped away. The first poem of *The Lost Hare* is typical in metrical exactness and final intensity: "millions / of compass-points of light, [...] one measure of sobriety, / one of delight."

Bogin's work is both exquisite, as in her "plum-coloured dusk", and razor-sharp. Her hawk is a "switch-blade". Her landscapes, in her own phrase, reveal history's "hard truth". Blackthorn's flower "like barbed wire [...] twists and turns / through this no-man's-land". Her terse lines on the World War One dead have searing rhymes "they seem younger [...] the years between us shorter, / and the war they fought in / never-ending slaughter".

The recalling of personal time, in Bogin's poems, has a memorable grace. She tests the limits of language, recording teenage bereavement greeted "without a word [...] our grief for you locked up inside the car". A lost son is imagined as an adult, breathing a lover's "cinnamon scent". But Bogin's art, in gently fading rhymes, registers the "hard truth" of death's distance: "tall and forthright / in the dark-enfolding night, first-born, stillborn son / passing by on the far side of life".

Her poetry, clear and direct, is never narrowly personal. The "lost hare" is "bedded down in the thoughts / and dreams I hoarded there". Each listener can add experience to that hoard. Bogin's poetry is its own place, but her particular patch of poetic earth can also become her readers' country.

Acclaimed children's poetry and radio plays fall within the territory of Chrissie Gittins's writing. Her first poem opens with unpretentious freshness, amongst geese: "the hollering came first". But the plainness of Gittins's ending is uncompromising: "this time I knew you would die". Her poems explore grief's strangeness: "I'll dress one night as you". They also celebrate daily heroism, as the old walk, indoors, with "head down against the wind". Gittins's metaphors are bold, with infectious desires, "to dip my finger / In the jar of life".

Gittins's fictional "King of Peru" "comforts himself with a rhyme". Her factual poems display winning, rocking rhythms. Their childhood reference is particularly touching in her account of a dead parent's possessions: "The green glass shone / that quarter to one, / making mahogany sizzle."

Her rhythms dance. Even death "can do the tango", while a mother is recalled by "the light fantastic / Of your love". Echoes of tongue-twisters are poignant in the account of Mary Anning, pioneering palaeontologist, reduced to "selling seashells by the shore".

Gittins speaks strongly in the voices of the overlooked dead, whether Pepys's mistress or a woman machine-breaker. With equal intensity, she focuses on beauty within her own life, such as "the peach flush / Of a bullfinch" outside the house she must sell. Her appealing poems reconnect a child's wide-awake senses with an adult's intelligence and passion. "Have you any idea how thick the dark can be?"

Cherry Smyth's poetry has an extraordinary quality, expressed in the title of her first poem: 'Transparency'. Its long, incantatory lines overflow fluidly: "In Japan, in a laboratory in the hills, a man is whispering to water [...] each isolated drop / seems to listen". Smyth's listener or reader is rewarded by remarkable variety. Formally, *Test, Orange* ranges from haiku to prose poems. It challenges the intellect, quoting Louise Bourgeois: "art is made of all / the things you desire that you say no to". It is deeply reflective: "The space between a death and a name is myth". But it also echoes a primitive rawness, including the parade-watchers' cry: "You homo scum!"

Test, Orange's rendering of its world is unflinching, admitting "the ash taste of Spain". Futures are glimpsed grimly: "riots for food / have already begun". But the poems are side-lit by beauty, noting, beside a sick relative, "a seam of bright moss / outlining the crazy paving". They are courageous, as when contemplating the sea: "this grief will not take me out". Endings are bravely colloquial: "There will be sun. It won't frighten us".

Smyth's lines on Héloïse are typically urgent and intense: "Love hangs in a hush around her, enclosing, chosen; [...] a trust in the best / in all that lives, that drives life's sweetness". She is a restless, prolific poet whose work pulses wonderfully with both sex and art: "bodies ringing like bells". But, throughout, her meaning remains transparent.

What do Sappho's words mean? Ask Dunmore's blackbird, Bogin's hare, Gitttins' bullfinch, Smyth's whispered waters. "The most beautiful thing on this dark earth" is what you love.

Alison Brackenbury's eighth collection, *Then*, will be published by Carcanet in April 2013.

ℬ

How Close We Came

DAVID MORLEY

Sean Borodale, *Bee Journal*, Cape, £10, ISBN 9780224097215;
Richard Meier, *Misadventure*, Picador, £9.99, ISBN 9781447208464;
Colm Keegan, *Don't Go There*, Salmon, £10, ISBN 9781908836069;
Sam Riviere, *81 Austerities*, Faber, £9.99, ISBN 9780571289035

I read Sean Borodale's *Bee Journal* out-of-doors and was continually brushing honey-bees from both the book and my hands ("bees batting this pen and poem's paper", as Borodale puts it). It was the cover picture, I imagine, rather than some encoded salsa at the entrance to language's hive. I have often thought you would need to *be* a bee to understand the language of their dance but Borodale, through entranced observation and intimate notation, is a worthy translator.

This is a book in which poems, like pollinators, are possessed by communal purpose. It is a journal of beekeeping that chronicles the life of a hive from a small nucleus on the first day to the capture of a swarm two years later:

> The air's innards have sprung apart.
> I am netted in trawls of strumming bee.
> Can I say
> what kind of halo absorbs me?   ('3rd July: Gift')

A single subject such as beekeeping might yield – in lesser hands – little more than thirteen ways of looking at a honeycomb. At worst, it could be some pseudoscientific lament. No such perils beset *Bee Journal*. It is gritty, wild and precise. Every sense of the poet is bent to the task of recording and responding. It is as much a psychic mission as it is a physical commission.

A journal is a place for styles to be hazarded. It is no place for (in a phrase borrowed from Ted Hughes) the goblins of literature. The unliterariness of Borodale's journal is the key to its realisation, its painting-by-words *en plein air*. The practice has much in common with the procedure by which Ted Hughes came to write *Moortown Diary* (or, for that matter, Alice Oswald came to write *Dart*). It is less palpably designed a creative act than it seems. As Hughes remarked in a recording about the farming poems of *Moortown*, his purpose was "to get the details down fresh, to make an archive of such details that might someday supply material for something more considered". Yet, in revisiting his poems in order to extract the 'literature', Hughes discovered he banished the "fresh, simple presence of the experience... so I let them lie in their rags and tatters". Sean Borodale, too, borrowing from bees and combing his field-notes, has left many of these poems in their rags and tatters, left his vision on its hinge and his mind's eye wide open. And the poems live urgently by their perfect imperfection, in their decisive non-poetryness. Sure as a perianth yields nectar and honey-bees hone it to honey, the tattered buzz of *Bee Journal* enacts a natural process of collection, concentration and accumulation that is – in a word – human:

> You, bee man, lifting a frame to light, count only numbers.
> You *are* human; what bees count must be more than parts.
> Breathe on them your dream of honey-smeared taste.
>
> They agitate and are in dream what sun pens.
>
> ('30th May: Examining Brood')

Richard Meier's *Misadventure* won the inaugural Picador Poetry Prize. I am very glad this inventive award brought his work to greater attention. His poetry is sharp, lovely and curiously graceful; his diction surprises by stealth and restraint, and his mind has something of the night about it, a nip of Robert Frost's "peck of the cold". Frost's friend Edward Thomas is an influence as is, dare I say, Meier's adroit editor. But Meier is his own poet and as fully-formed in his written humanity as Borodale.

Meier's poems about his wife, children and garden – all the invisible, imperative ceremonies of grace and gracelessness – are skilfully realised, as is his own self-distrust (it is intriguing how absent a figure the poet seems to be when he is in his own poems). Yet at moments, in 'Three Weeks to Go' and 'Canute Explains', Meier bursts upon us with something quite other to our expectations. This is one of those rare books that will cheer without patronising, and show you how to speak past grief and silence while still holding all that grief and all that silence.

All writing is performance. There is no serious, organic distinction between spoken and written word. If you know the Irish poet Colm Keegan's work from his exceptional performances on YouTube you should not be surprised by how deftly his poetry transfers to the silent stage of a book. *Don't Go There* is lively, provocative and genuine. Its strengths on the page are directness, frankness and a challenging lyricism. He portrays Dublin in a similar vein to how Sean Borodale portrays his bee-hives: no exaggeration, no reaching for myths or for non-human vacuum, no literary bullshit.

The core of his work is a humane understanding beyond the clichés of vulnerability and powerlessness. Keegan is a keen observer of reality. Like most real people, he does not do distance. Very often in these poems Keegan achieves the most terrific sense of drama from the familiar. In 'The Wind of the Spin', two cars crash in front of the writer "as if tied to the spire / of the church they passed / like kids swinging on a maypole / after smashing into each other". The accident is described in slow-motion, with a kind of horribly recognisable, savage bliss we cannot but help feel when we are not the victim:

> So that me and all the other people
> standing nearby feel
> nothing but the wind
> of the spin on our faces
> like a kiss.
>
> We all bear witness as
> two men stumble out of
> the wreckage to stare at
> each other in disbelief.
> Constellations of broken glass
> beneath their feet.
>
> Nobody wanting to dole out blame.
> Nobody second guessing
> the near miss.
>
> *Are you alright?*
> *Are you alright?*
> they say.
> While trying to reason this.
> How close we came.

Reading Sam Riviere's *81 Austerities* (and his associated website), I was reminded of John Cage's 1949 'Lecture on Nothing' in which he stated, "I have nothing to say / and I am saying it / and that is poetry / as I needed it".

Riviere's diction is inflected through a number of poets who say nothing and everything beautifully. What Riviere's book is remarkable for is its style, for its jettisoning of style.

It begins with subject: "Austerity was named the word of the year by Merriam-Webster in 2010". It 'deals' with the funding cuts of today as Peter Reading 'dealt' with the funding cuts of the 1980s:

> I can see that things have gotten pretty bad
> our way of life threatened by financiers
> assortments of phoneys and opportunists
> and very soon the things we cherish most
> will likely be taken from us the wine
> from our cellars our silk gowns and opium ('Cuts')

But this is not a book about actual austerities. To the author's credit, he has pointed towards them as the catalyst, a stimulus for a work of complex art. To that end *81 Austerities* is not without considerable beauty, attack and panache:

> Who wouldn't rather be watching
> a film about werewolves instead
> of composing friends' funeral playlists? ('Regular Black')

Yet the austerity in this book is one of style – of no-style at all. Like plucking one string of the blue guitar it becomes all-style, a purified mania. The apoetical becomes apolitical. Even by modish inversion this no-style presents a kind of purified inaction. And that is what I think is the author's honest, artistic intention. That is what Riviere wants to deliver. For him, it would be indefensible to believe a poetry book could alter policy, save lives, avert harm to the vulnerable. The truth is, of course, this book does not set out to do so. Why should it? How could it?

Nobody who really suffers in the ongoing and oncoming austerities will read this book or this magazine because they are largely invisible to the dominant cultures that make and read poetry. Yet the vulnerable are poetry. In some ways you could argue *81 Austerities* is appropriating the terms of their distress. In other ways this book could be said to be the most appropriate of poetic responses to our empty political and cultural values. We are all in this emptiness – together.

Each of these books under review is a debut collection. Reviewers usually parade that message early, disarming reception with a white flag. But these four good poets need no such shelter. They are all yours. You know what to do with them.

David Morley's next poetry collection from Carcanet in 2013 is *The Gypsy and the Poet*. He currently teaches at Warwick University. www.davidmorley.org.uk

International

Poetry Prize €1,000

Judge: Paul Durcan

Word limit is 300. Entry fee €14.
Closes 28 Feb '13.

Last winner: Martin Childs.

Submissions by post or online.
Read the full details on

www.fishpublishing.com

The ten best poems will be
published in the 2013
Fish Anthology

[See website for mentoring]

Fish Publishing, Durrus,
Bantry, Co Cork, Ireland
info@fishpublishing.com

poetry london

On the departure of the current editor in spring 2013, Poetry London will seek to appoint a **FREELANCE POETRY EDITOR** to join the editorial team. Application packs may be downloaded from the website www.poetrylondon.co.uk or requested by email: admin@poetrylondon.co.uk

Deadline for applications: **18 JANUARY 2013**

Fragility in Shadow

ROB A. MACKENZIE

Valerie Laws, *All That Lives*, Red Squirrel, £6.99, ISBN 9781906700430;
Omar Sabbagh, *Waxed Mahogany*, Agenda, £9.99, ISBN 9781908527011;
Todd Swift, *When All My Disappointments Came at Once*,
Tightrope, £12.50, ISBN 9781926663451;
Ghassan Zaqtan, trans. Fady Joudah, *Like a Straw Bird It Follows Me,
and Other Poems*, Yale, £18.99, ISBN 9780300173161

All four of these collections relate, in some measure, an autobiographical response to loss – whether of life, memory, identity or health – but their modes of expression could hardly be more diverse.

Valerie Laws draws largely on narrative to reflect on her parents' illnesses and deaths, followed by a sequence on dissection. Humorous poems on dating lighten the mood with varying success. The opening poems on her mother's dementia are moving, but quite prose-like, and it was only by the fifth poem, 'The Incredible Shrinking Brain', that I got a sense of a poetic (as opposed to storytelling) intelligence. The words of the poem's first section are gradually removed in six subsequent versions so that surviving phrases and encroaching white space mirror the onset of dementia. In the final section, only a single word, "gone", remains.

Laws's residencies in pathology and neuroscience research units have produced some fine work. 'A Litter of Moons' presents foetal specimens in a pathology museum. In contrast to "cute" film aliens:

> we dropped into your world to gasps
> and screams, at how nature riffs
> on your forked symmetry, your skin
> with its certainty of inside, outside.

The voice becomes tragic as it addresses the viewer (and reader) and confesses it hadn't realised "how you'd fear us, flinch / from our delicate, audacious difference". Laws doesn't flinch from lurid, eerily fascinating description, but the poems which work best also find a new angle on human anxieties and fears, such as the tense 'Rat Brain: Waving Not Drowning' in which a sliver of rat brain continues unconsciously to emit waves and "each / Tide of waves newly detected, washes us closer / To what we don't yet know."

Omar Sabbagh's first two collections centred on desire, identity, metaphysics, and family past and present. *Waxed Mahogany* develops these themes. It is highly stylised work, frequently combining end-rhyme with fragmented confessional utterance and Muldoonian sonic gymnastics. Sabbagh's vocabulary is rich and his tone elevated, as in 'A Horse, A Horse':

> There's something awry in the corner of the room –
> As though a fountain slides bluely through to a sea's choppy dream,
> As though kindness were a lucid idiom
> for the acid scream
> Of cliff-like crag, its shriek, and the ocean-deep obscene.

What seems most awry here is the overwriting: "acid scream", "ocean-deep obscene" and the "crimson wings less chorus or cue" of the following stanza undermine any subtle sense of mystery that may otherwise have been generated. Sabbagh has a great ear for word-music, but this intoxication can lead him to settle for some dubious constructions. It also can generate delightful collisions, such as in 'His Eyebrows', when "the arch pen"

> Is what this world-whole masque – a roughness – demands.
> Like bran. Brawn. Born. Borne. Eyebrows: nut-brown.
>
> Ought. Can.

I admired Sabbagh's intensity and ambition but questioned whether he was articulating much of significance. His "livid amps of hurt" ('No Church') too often seemed veiled in insubstantial prolixity.

The title of Todd Swift's seventh collection, *When All My Disappointments Came at Once*, might seem melodramatic, but sterility, depression and esophagitis are enough to take their toll on anyone. The resulting poems pave a *via negativa* through times when sources of hope seem absent. In 'God has left us like a girl', a girl walks by, "leaving us alone to pray / that tomorrow, again, she will / deign to, lightly, reappear." Swift's manipulation of rhythm here is impressive. With "again" and the heavy, infinitive-splitting "lightly", he transforms an otherwise wistful hope into something akin to desperation.

In 'After riding the escalator back', Swift is in a mall, returning a broken watch, accompanied by his wife "who loves me and worries for // the sorrow that ticks away / inside the case of my self-schism." The kindness of the watch merchant also makes an impression on him, but Swift still sees himself as

> a cog that clicks
> upon another toothed gear

> stymied again, under the magnifying
> glass, still unable to be pried free.

That is a tragically perfect image for depression. The poem flits gracefully between narrative, metaphor and commentary. Swift makes it look easy here and in a number of strong poems such as 'Song in a Time of Inflation', 'Sonnet' and 'Slieve Donard' in which a faint lighthouse is "a comic smudge of hope / pressed like an insect // into the book of night", a stark image from this powerful and painfully honest odyssey through brokenness, love and recovery.

Ghassan Zaqtan is a Palestinian writer who explores familiar themes of memory and absence in entirely unfamiliar ways. *Like a Straw Bird It Follows Me, and Other Poems* houses a complete collection from 2008 and selections from 1998 and 2003. Fady Joudah's translations from Arabic read well as poems in English – complexly fragmented, suggestive and vivid.

In the 1998 selection, *Luring the Mountain*, the dead dance in the grass "as if they were the garden's motive / or its meditation" ('The Dead in the Garden'). Zaqtan is determined not to draw simplistic conclusions from suffering, as he angrily makes clear in 'The Islands':

> Noon gathers
> like a stabbed horse
> while the poets lean over seductive wisdom
> pick it out of the commoners' death.

Biography in Charcoal, the 2003 selection, specifically addresses personal and collective exile, loss and violence. In 'An Enemy Comes Down the Hill', the generic "enemy" becomes

> fragility in shadow,
> the Jewish man with a long mustache
> who resembles the dead Arabs here.

No longer a faceless threat, then, but a fragile human being like oneself. Like one's dead.

In 2008's *Like a Straw Bird it Follows Me*, Zaqtan explores what he calls a "whirling in my head" ('Alone and the River Follows Me'): a litany of scattered things that might provide pretexts for making sense of loss and memory, and for why a poet might find it necessary to write about them. He carries narratives like luggage and can't abandon them because

> Something wrong happened there at the starting line
> a minor error that accumulates its dark with the patience
> and perseverance of the dead. ('As If He Were She')

Words and phrases link poems and ideas together, not as mere language games but as ever-deepening resonance. With each reading, I found myself struck by echoes I'd missed before, and I am unable to do this wonderful book justice in the space available here. It is rich, exciting, vital, humane work that puts everything else I've read this year in the shade.

Rob A. Mackenzie lives in Edinburgh. His last publication was the pamphlet *Fleck and the Bank* (Salt, 2012). His second full collection, *The Good News*, will be published by Salt in 2013.

Paul Muldoon's 'A Giraffe' in a stunning limited edition

To mark the occasion of the 2012 Poetry Society Annual Lecture, the Poetry Society has produced a limited edition print of Paul Muldoon's poem 'A Giraffe'

Featuring a delightfully witty illustration by the artist John Vernon Lord, the edition was printed by Phil Abel of Hand & Eye letterpress studio, London. The print is published in a strictly limited edition, making it the perfect Christmas gift.

Full price: £12
Poetry Society members: £7

Signed copies are available at no extra charge while stocks last.

THE POETRY SOCIETY

BUY ONLINE at www.poetrysociety.org.uk

Family, Relationships, Perspectives

SARAH WARDLE

Julia Copus, *The World's Two Smallest Humans*,
Faber, £9.99, ISBN 9780571284573;
Beverley Bie Brahic, *White Sheets*, CB editions, £7.99, ISBN 9780956735959;
Gerry McGrath, *Rooster*, Carcanet, £9.95, ISBN 9781847771162;
David Herd, *All Just*, Carcanet, £9.95, ISBN 9781847771636

Julia Copus's latest collection, *The World's Two Smallest Humans*, is a deeply moving account of loss of self-confidence, caused by an unsatisfactory relationship, which leads her to reliance on medical science, IVF and a distrust of her own womanhood, yet ends with the hope of natural procreation: "By and by with the push of the wash / I'll usher you in".

The book opens with a backtrack to a recovery point at which a relationship did not end: "the street, in the moments after, does not shrink / to the slam of a door, the flare of an engine". She can say with hindsight: "tell me it's already too late to warn them". The mirror poem, popular as a school exercise in the seventies and eighties, and ubiquitous in school magazines, is a form she has used before and returns to here in nostalgic poems about retirement, unemployment and the moment when a former lover invited her to be a kept woman: "I had only meant to stay for a week".

'Impossible As It Seems' is a blend of Auden and Kennelly, making the point, as Auden does in 'Musée des Beaux Arts', that the world carries on whatever tragedies befall individuals, and ending with Kennelly's inspired exhortation to 'Begin again', yet without his contagious optimism. 'Now Winter Is In Me' echoes Dunn's 'On Roofs of Terry Street', focusing on the visual uplift of shining slates, yet where Dunn uses this as an epiphany of effort, Copus deploys the image as one of freeze and frigidity. 'This Silence Between Us' is reminiscent of Pierpoint's 'This Dead Relationship', except that Copus wants to resuscitate the body she imagines occupying the mattress space between her and her withdrawn partner. In 'The Orange Rug' it is her brothers she yearns for, as she revisits her childhood home. Yet in 'Memories, when Fixed' there is a glimmer of insight and a way forward, where, comparing difficult experiences to scars of the skin, she conjectures:

"Perhaps we could even / learn to love them".

She further explores leisure and the affairs of the heart through the example of a man Mozart deployed to keep his pregnant wife sweet. The atmosphere is pure Chekhov, the poem filmed through the lens of a costume drama that lacks passion. Lines such as, "The master snaps his fingers and we jump", say it all. There is an echo of Armitage's 'Zoom!' in the lines, "O there is much, Anton, more needful to the spirit / even than music, though he will not have it", but the energy of Armitage is replaced with apathy, the chutzpah with listlessness. Elsewhere she voices lack of fulfilment through the legend of Hero longing for Leander, as she paces the shore in a storm, before going back into her hutch.

The closing sequence chronicles the poet's unsuccessful forays into IVF. Perhaps one reason for the failure is in the line, "Now they drink to the dregs of their coffee". Plath's 'Mushrooms' is invoked to depict the growing embryos, an indication of the sense of invasion the mechanised process makes her feel, rather than the natural love that could have been. The fact she thinks the clinical and kitsch treatment chair's "purple arms reach out / for her" shows just how much warmth her lover is not providing. Although she compares the failure of the procedure to autumn leaves and prefaces her book with a quote from Hilary Mantel, Copus is only in her early forties and this fine poet has years of creation to come.

Beverley Bie Brahic's second collection, *White Sheets*, opens with a woman hanging washing, sheltered from the realities of a wider world, and closes with laundry drying in a remote landscape. There are moving elegies for her father, whose war stories form vicarious experiences of life beyond the home, as do references to Thucydides. Dry versions of a French author are interspersed with poems on an uneventful reunion, a teapot, kitchen, garden and bedroom scenes, but it is in livelier poems centred on Eve, travel and her relationship with her mother that the book takes off and generates an original voice. She records her and her mother's joint effort to move on after her father's death, their scattering of his ashes, co-dependency, division of his property, sale of their accumulated junk, her visits to her mother in hospital, her solitude as sole occupant of house and garden. The white sheets seem sails of a boat she voyages in alone.

By contrast Gerry McGrath's second book, *Rooster*, is full of love and family life. Despite their brevity, these poems are affirming: "I know but I don't know / what every night allows me / why every day brings only light". At times clarity is sacrificed and the poet over-reaches into pretentious phrasing, or veiled associations, but at others he scales heights of expression:

"So I ask / if the present is sadness / what is the past'. In 'I Hope' he describes the future of poetry lying where lyric and environmental concerns meet, and a world view at once hopeful and bleak: "In my son's blue gaze / a terrible clarity confers grace / while honesty like a vulture / circles overhead".

David Herd's second collection, *All Just*, reaches beyond personal lyrics to voice a man of Kent's views on a county of sea-defences, immigration points, the Dover Immigration Removal Centre, and the free migrations of gulls overhead. Justice is a key theme from the kangaroo court of bail hearings to the plight of a young refugee mother and child: "if he has a bail hearing – / which he is not entitled to attend – / though his lawyer is, / and the Judge is, / and a representative of the Home Office is – / the bail hearing – / imagine – / is officially un- / recorded". The changing registers and discourses of his writing, his cut-ups and repetitions, invite us to question the authority of law and language. There is also the sense in which we are all just human, mere mortals, but inconsequential.

Sarah Wardle's three books are *Fields Away*, shortlisted for a Forward prize, *Score!* and *A Knowable World*. She currently works as a creative writing tutor at Morley College, London.

STROKESTOWN
INTERNATIONAL **POETRY FESTIVAL**
AN INVITATION TO POETRY

The 2013 Strokestown International Poetry Award
For a single poem in English not exceeding 70 lines.

First Prize: €3000.
Second Prize: €1500. Third Prize: €1000.

Judges: Michael Schmidt and Iggy McGovern.
Closing date: January 25th 2013.

Part of the Strokestown International Poetry Festival,
Roscommon, Ireland, May 3rd-6th 2013.
Directed by Martin Dyar.

Entry details and updates: www.strokestownpoetry.org

CONTRIBUTORS

Elmi Ali is a Somali poet, fiction writer and dramatist, based in Manchester. **Mir Mahfuz Ali**'s first collection is due from Seren in 2014. **Ahimsa Timoteo Bodhrán** is the author of *Antes y después del Bronx: Lenapehoking*. **Ivy Alvarez**'s second collection is forthcoming from Seren. **Rowyda Amin**'s poems appear in *Ten: New Poets Spread the Word* (Bloodaxe). **Charlotte Ansell**'s poetry collections *you were for the poem* and *After Rain* are published by Flipped Eye. **Dzifa Benson** writes poems, short stories and radio plays. She has written for *The Guardian*, the BBC and the Royal Opera House. **Jay Bernard**'s work appears in *Out of Bounds*, *In Their Own Words* and *The Salt Book of Younger Poets*. **Yemisi Blake** is an artist, producer and researcher. **Jemma Borg** won the New Writing Ventures Award for Poetry in 2007 and is included in *Lung Jazz, Young British Poets for Oxfam* (Cinnamon Press, 2012). **Jo Brandon** is the author of *Phobia* (Valley Press). **Kayo Chingonyi**'s pamphlet, *Some Bright Elegance*, is out from Salt. **Sophie Clarke** is working towards a first collection. **Geraldine Clarkson** is featured in *This Line Is Not For Turning: An Anthology of Contemporary British Prose Poetry* (Cinnamon, 2011). **Suzanne Conway** has published widely in magazines and is studying for a PhD. **Edward Doegar** is working towards a first collection. **Suzi Feay** was Literary Editor of the *Independent on Sunday*, and is a critic, blogger and lecturer. **Rody Gorman** edits the anthology *An Guth*. His latest collection, *Sweeney: An Intertonguing*, is forthcoming. **Matthew Gregory** received an Eric Gregory award in 2010. **Katie Hale** is currently working on her first collection. **Ishion Hutchinson**'s first collection, *Far District*, won the PEN/Joyce Osterweil Award. He teaches English at Cornell University. **Nabila Jameel** is a British Pakistani poet. **Anthony Joseph** is the author of four collections of poetry. **Valerie Laws**'s latest collection is *All That Lives* (Red Squirrel Press). **Nicholas Laughlin** is Editor of *The Caribbean Review of Books*. **Hannah Lowe**'s first collection, *Chick*, will be published in 2013. **Nick Makoha** represented Uganda at Poetry Parnassus. His work appears in *Ten* (Bloodaxe). **Sophie Mayer** co-edited *Catechism: Poems for Pussy Riot*. Her most recent collections are *The Private Parts of Girls* (Salt) and *Kiss Off* (Oystercatcher). **Simon McCormack**'s poems have appeared in *Magma*, *Cyprus Well Writer Bites* and at the Bath Independent Literature Festival. **Abegail Morley**'s *How to Pour Madness into a Teacup* was shortlisted for the Forward Prize for Best First Collection. Her second book is *Snow Child* and a pamphlet, *A German Tale*, is forthcoming. **Katrina Naomi**'s first collection *The Girl with the Cactus Handshake* was shortlisted for the London New Poetry Award. **Tolu Ogunlesi**'s poetry has appeared in *Wasafiri*, *London Magazine*, *Sable* and *Magma*. **Diriye Osman**'s book of short stories, *Fairytales For Lost Children*, is due in 2013. **Moya Pacey**'s first collection, *The Wardrobe*, was published by Ginninderra Press Australia. **Jocelyn Page**'s pamphlet is *smithereens* (tall-lighthouse). **Roger Robinson**'s books include *Suitcase* and *Suckle*. **Brigid Rose**'s novel, *The City of Lists*, won the Crocus Books North West Novel Writers' competition. **Jacqueline Saphra**'s first collection, *The Kitchen of Lovely Contraptions*, was nominated for the Aldeburgh First Collection Prize 2011. **Richard Scott** won the Wasafiri New Writing Prize 2011 and was a Jerwood/ Arvon Poetry Mentee. **Warsan Shire**'s *Teaching My Mother How To Give Birth* was published by Flipped Eye in 2011. **Dorothea Smartt**'s two collections are *Connecting Medium* and *Ship Shape*, both Peepal Tree Press. **Caroline Smith** is finishing her third collection of poems, *The Immigration Handbook*. **Steve Tasane** is Writer-in-Residence for the Dickens 2012 Bicentennial Celebrations. **Marvin Thompson** has a seven sonnet corona due for publication in *Wasafiri*.

Discover a world of beautiful illustrated editions with The Folio Society

SINCE 1947, The Folio Society has become one of England's most creative publishing houses. In our 5-year history, we have published an astonishing range of works; from *Moby-Dick* to *The Wonderful Wizard of Oz*, and from the *Bible* to *The Hitchhiker's Guide to the Galaxy*. Our current list includes nearly 400 works of fiction, biography, history, science, children's literature, poetry, philosophy, travel and more.

Books that are beautiful inside and out

Our bindings are crafted in buckram, cotton, silk or leather, and blocked with beautiful designs. We commission new illustrations from artists of the calibre of Quentin Blake, Charles van Sandwyk and Tom Phillips RA. And our editions feature specially commissioned introductions by leading writers such as Umberto Eco for Jacques le Goff's *Medieval Civilisation* and Michael Cunningham, Pulitzer prize-winning author of *The Hours*, for *Mrs Dalloway*.

There are hundreds of beautifully bound and illustrated Folio editions to discover on our website including the *Selected Poems & Prose* of Gerard Manley Hopkins, the *Selected Poems of Robert Frost* plus *A Folio Anthology of Poetry* and *The Crimson Fairy Book,* both of which are introduced by Poet Laureate Carol Ann Duffy. Visit us now, and you're entitled to FREE delivery of your order.

Go to www.foliosociety.com / tps

Binding design *The Selected Poems & Prose* of Gerard Manley Hopkins

Head and tail bands   Exquisite typographic design

Illustration by Grahame Baker-Smith from Carlo Collodi's *Pinocchio*

FREE DELIVERY WITH YOUR FIRST ORDER

Beautiful books from The Folio Society start from just £19.95. Browse our exquisite collection now at www.foliosociety.com / tps and you're entitled to FREE delivery of your order, simply use code FRP at checkout.

Visit us at www.foliosociety.com / tps

THE FOLIO SOCIETY
Beautiful illustrated books

Colin Sky   User ID: CWA72

*Anthony Knight is an award-winning poet who has
had scores of poems published in various periodicals and
anthologies on both sides of the Atlantic.*

His poetry is now available on KINDLE.

THE DEBRIS FIELD

(Collected Shorter Poems) at £0.77

BEYOND THE TERMINUS

(Collected Longer Poems) at £0.77

'A bagpipe on a Breton morning throws
Me back to Highland lochs and wind-hung crows.'
— *Madeleine Moments*

'...For beauty from the beautiful comes easily.
Making art from ugliness is the better test.'
— *Modigliani's Mistress*

'All States and Princes have a taste for slaughter.
They use our son and flag-waving daughter.'
— *A Vision of Murdered Children*

'Telescopes for stars, microscopes for cells.
How are we studied and what would be seen?'
— *At Canary Wharf*

'You attempt to trick me with Narcissus.
But I echo his name back to you, you.'
— *Playing Lovers*

'Full stops can occur, outside
Grammar, in the middle of.'
— *Sentences*

'Shakespeare in a fever throws off his robe,
And asks: "How much did 'Tempest' take at the Globe?"'
— *Famous Last Words (As Should Be)*

Why not take advantage of vintage wine for the price of plonk?